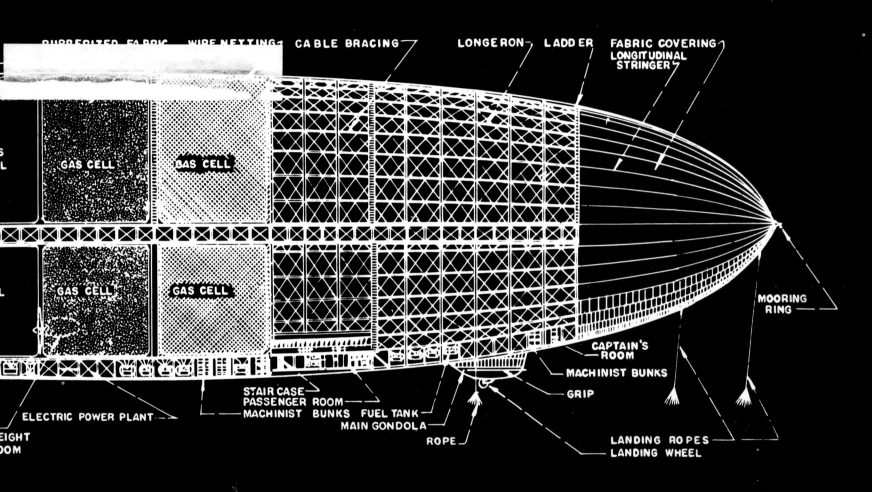

RUBBERIZED FABRIC   WIRE NETTING   CABLE BRACING   LONGERON   LADDER   FABRIC COVERING
LONGITUDINAL STRINGER

GAS CELL   GAS CELL

GAS CELL   GAS CELL

MOORING RING

CAPTAIN'S ROOM

MACHINIST BUNKS

GRIP

STAIR CASE
PASSENGER ROOM
MACHINIST BUNKS   FUEL TANK
MAIN GONDOLA

ELECTRIC POWER PLANT

ROPE

LANDING ROPES
LANDING WHEEL

EIGHT
OOM

Side view of the *Hindenburg*.

First published in the United States in 1979 by
Holt, Rinehart and Winston, 383 Madison Ave., New York, N.Y. 10017.
Library of Congress Catalog Card Number 78–68317
ISBN: 03–046451–X
Printed in Great Britain
10 9 8 7 6 5 4 3 2 1

Other books by
LEN DEIGHTON

Non-fiction
FIGHTER: The True Story of
the Battle of Britain

War fiction
BOMBER
DECLARATIONS OF WAR
SS-GB

Spy fiction
THE IPCRESS FILE
HORSE UNDER WATER
FUNERAL IN BERLIN
BILLION DOLLAR BRAIN
AN EXPENSIVE PLACE TO DIE
SPY STORY
YESTERDAY'S SPY
CATCH A FALLING SPY

Novel
CLOSE-UP

The destruction of the
German airship L19 as
reconstructed for a
wartime propaganda film.
See p. 32.

LEN DEIGHTON & ARNOLD SCHWARTZMAN
AIRSHIPWRECK

HOLT, RINEHART AND WINSTON NEW YORK

This map sites the principal wrecks mentioned in this book.

North Pole

Courla

Fanö Island

Yorkshire Moors

Tondern

Barrow

Little Wigborough

Heligoland Island

R. Elbe

Llangefni

Hull

Ahlhorn

Nordholz

Berlin

Noble County

Lakehurst

Theberton

Teutoburg Forest

Düsseldorf

London

Ostend

Limburg

Tiefenort

Atlantic

Evere

Weilburg

Thames Estuary

Bruges

Frankfurt

Sunnyvale

Beauvais

Schweinfurt

Stuttgart

Meudon

Luneville

Echterdingen

Gonesse

Bourbonne-les-Bains

Kisslegg

Friedrichshafen

Bodensee

Map by QED.

INTRODUCTION

The eyes of my two young sons search the skies looking for an airship. They have seen jet planes, double-decker buses, old cars and even an old sailing ship. They recognised them from the pictures that in my house clutter the walls, floors, tables and chairs. Our neighbour flies a replica of von Richthofen's red Triplane, so that is no less real to them than the steam-roller that arrives after the water pipes are laid for a new house in the village. But they will never see the great silver shape of a rigid airship floating in the sky, as they float on the walls of my room. The rigid airship has gone for ever.

And yet within living memory few men doubted that lighter-than-air craft were the only practical air transport for passengers and freight. The invention of the steam engine encouraged men to think that powered flight was possible. The development of the aeroplane was slow: the way in which these 'heavier-than-air' machines could lift into the sky was mysterious, and for most people it remains so. The problem of getting an airship to fly was obvious to all. Hydrogen is lighter than air; manufacture it and it will float upwards; hold on to it and you'll rise too. In 1887 the electrolytic production of aluminium provided girders from which a very lightweight rigid structure could be built. Inside it, hydrogen-filled gas bags could be fixed.

In 1888 Mr Daimler offered a two horse-power engine to an airship designer. It needed only the incredible Graf von Zeppelin and the airship – or Zeppelin – was a practical proposition. By 1914 air travel had become almost commonplace for Germans. The Zeppelins had by that time carried 37,250 passengers over 90,000 miles of air route without death or injury to any of them. There were regular scheduled flights during the summer months and for a brief period in 1912 a daily air-mail postal service was provided for several towns.

These Zeppelin passengers could enjoy an excellent cold lunch, with fine wines, relax in their wicker armchairs, with their feet on the carpet, watching the German countryside unroll at a steady 45 miles per hour. When, in 1914, there came the news that the first passenger-carrying aeroplane service had started, the airship men were not impressed. Why should they be? The aeroplanes only operated from Tampa to St Petersburg, in Florida, USA, the passengers had to dress in heavy flying gear, and there was only one passenger per aeroplane. It was a dangerous, uncomfortable and unprofitable adventure.

For many years airships dominated the air routes. By 1936 the regular scheduled airship service between Germany and Rio de Janeiro and the airship service between Germany and New York were still the only transatlantic air routes. No aeroplane could perform such a task. The following year the *Hindenburg* burned and decades of accident-free airship flights were obliterated by awesome film and photo of the burning Zeppelin. And yet the aeroplane could still not provide air routes across the Atlantic. It wasn't until 1939 that heavier-than-air machines carried fare-paying passengers on the Atlantic route – a full twenty years after the R34 airship had crossed. Even then the aeroplanes could not equal the airship's flight; they had intermediate stops at Bermuda and the Azores (or Newfoundland and Ireland on the northerly route). It wasn't until the middle 1950s that airlines offered passengers a direct service across the Atlantic.

For me the airship has a magic that the aeroplane cannot replace. The size is awesome, the shape Gothic; a pointed arch twirled into a tracery of aluminium. And the reality is not disappointing. No one present ever forgot the day a concert pianist

Graf von Zeppelin.

Gottlieb Daimler.

sat down and gave his fellow passengers a recital while the airship moved through the cloudy skies of the Atlantic. There were special trips too. In 1929 the *Graf Zeppelin* took some lucky passengers from the very severe European winter for a gentle, non-stop flight round the eastern Mediterranean. The schedule was prepared so that they breakfasted over the Riviera, saw Athens at dawn and the Holy Land by moonlight. The airships usually flew very low: the ground was so close and the engines so quiet that it was not unusual to hear voices from below and dogs barking at the strange silvery shape.

And if the sights were memorable, the comfort was no less so. Famous chefs prepared the food in well-equipped, if cramped, galleys. On the Orient Flight in 1929 the twenty-four passengers consumed 160 bottles of spirits and 63 quarts of excellent wines.

The *Hindenburg* airship had over 5,000 square feet of carpeted passenger-space. There was a lounge, library and writing room and a promenade from which huge windows gave a view of the ground. After dark the promenade was curtained off so that the night landscape could be seen.

So where did the dream go wrong? No two experts exactly agree. Certainly time was the airship's

enemy. 'Airships breed like elephants and aeroplanes like rabbits,' said C. G. Grey, editor of the *Aeroplane*, in 1928, rightly predicting that evolution must favour aeroplanes.

In another sense, time was the airship's enemy. The *Hindenburg* could move a 20-ton payload a distance of 8,000 miles. Thirty years later an aeroplane – the Lockheed C-130E Hercules – could move only 12.5 tons a distance of 3,400 miles. The superiority of the aeroplane lies in its cruising speed of 312 knots compared with the airship's mere 62 knots. Money invested in the aeroplane can be earned by several flights while the airship makes only one. This leaves aside the dangers of airship operations, the hazards of hydrogen, the cost of helium and the necessity to protect airships on the ground by means of gigantic hangars. (The twin hangar at Lakehurst, New Jersey, covers 8 acres of ground and is taller than either the Statue of Liberty or Nelson's Column, and it is not the largest hangar.)

But the airship remains one of the greatest triumphs of structural engineering the world has ever seen. Hydrogen is lighter than air, but only marginally so. It was almost impossible to make a rigid airship that was light enough to lift into the sky, yet strong enough to endure the forces of nature it would encounter there.

In this book, with the help of experts, I have told the story of the airship's failure. It shows the daunting task that the airship designer faced. Perhaps all simple acts of faith bear an imprint of absurdity, and you'll find it here. But the book is intended as a tribute to the master builders and their aluminium marvels. This generation of engineers dared to build their cathedrals in the sky; no wonder then that so few of them stayed there.

Len Deighton
1978

Left: *Hindenburg* over New York, 1937.

AIRSHIPWRECK

In flying, as in the other arts and sciences, theorists have always outnumbered practicians. There has never been a lack of designs for flying machines, although few were built, and fewer lifted from the ground. There were claims from China, Portugal and Russia too but as far as history records, Frenchmen flew first, in Paris, in 1783.

The first flyers were in a balloon carried upwards by warmed air, but in that same year other men ascended in a balloon that used hydrogen. For more than a century, the only flying machines were to be those that were lighter than air.

The problem of making an envelope that was both very light and gas-proof was solved by the Robert brothers, who were already selling a very fine, and extremely light-weight, rubberised silk. Before tailoring it into an airship for the Duke of Chartres they were prospering from the strictly illegal manufacture of contraceptives. Now they made a gigantic fish shape that would swim through the air. So carefully did they make its double envelope that when the airship flew on 6 July 1784 there were no leaks. And there was no way of valving the gas out. The airship ascended and would have burst had not the Duke himself poked a hole in it with his flagstaff. It descended into the park at Meudon.

The flying machines inspired rage and fear. An unmanned hydrogen balloon, sent up on a test flight from the Champs de Mars, Paris, landed at Gonesse, about fifteen miles away, where the villagers assaulted it with farm implements.

But not all crowds were so frightened of the flying machines. An airship, 130 feet long, designed and built under the direction of the Comte de Lennox in 1834, was torn to pieces by enraged onlookers just because she didn't rise into the air.

The design of the hydrogen balloon remains unchanged, but men wanted to power and steer their flying machines. Some dirigibles were powered by steam and by electricity but it was Herr Daimler's petrol engine that made flight possible.

«WÖLFERT»

A Berlin clergyman was the first man to fit a petrol engine to an airship. Encouraged by early tests, he modified the engine with a vaporiser of his own design – a platinum tube heated to incandescence by an open flame.

It was a fine June evening in 1897 when Dr Wölfert made his flight from Tempelhof, Berlin. The onlookers included many foreign officials, fellow aviators and technicians. Some of them were

Left: Gonesse: villagers attack an unmanned balloon.

Right: Dr Wölfert, a Berlin clergyman, with his airship in 1897.

alarmed to see the jet of flame from his engine. It was so close to the envelope, with its 28,000 cubic feet of explosive gas, but Dr Wölfert assured them it was normal.

At about seven that evening the airship ascended. She was 91 feet long, and by the time she climbed to about 3,000 feet she was being watched from almost every street in Berlin. The first sign of trouble was a shred of fabric trailing behind. Then there was a flicker of fire and an explosion as the airship was engulfed in flame. Some spectators thought they heard a scream. Blazing pieces of wreckage fell into the streets of Berlin. Scarcely recognisable amongst them were the charred remains of Dr Wölfert and his engineer.

«SCHWARZ»

During the latter half of the nineteenth century, a new miracle metal came on sale – aluminium. David Schwarz decided to make his entire airship from it. Perhaps she would have flown, but the problems of filling the metal envelope with gas proved too much. During the slow process of filling it, some internal bracing wires snapped, and the metal-clad airship collapsed.

Schwarz made another one but died before it flew. This time the more successful craft lifted into the air to the extent of a rope that tethered it. The rope snapped and, as the airship rose, her driving belt broke. Disconnected from her 12 h.p. Daimler engine, the airship floated on the breeze. The pilot panicked. He opened the gas release valve and the airship crashed to the ground and collapsed. The pilot jumped clear but the airship rolled away and the thin metal structure tore itself to pieces.

«LZ1»

The first of the Zeppelins. In July 1900, when Count von Zeppelin was 62 years old, the first Zeppelin was ready to fly. She was bigger and better than any previous machine and, as she was taken out of her floating shed on Lake Constance (Bodensee), there was a gasp of surprise from the assembled crowd. She had a capacity of about 400,000 cubic feet and two 12 h.p. Daimler engines, each driving two propellers.

The Count, a rotund old gentleman with a military bearing and a large walrus moustache, removed his smart, white, yachting cap and offered a short prayer. Then he climbed into the boat-like gondola with two other passengers, while two mechanics attended the engines. The Technical Director refused to fly with them on the grounds that his insurance had not come through.

A handling party of local firemen and a gymnas-

Left: The *Schwarz* airship's design was too far ahead of the technology available.

Right: LZ1 (Luftschiff Zeppelin No. 1) used a floating hangar anchored in Lake Constance. This photograph is of the very first flight in July 1900.

tic club released the mooring ropes. Those at the rear were not quick enough, and the airship lifted away with her nose in the air.

To level off the airship a heavy weight was winched forward. This primitive device worked the first time but then jammed. Nose down, the airship nearly touched the water but ballast was released and she rose again. The small engines and the slow, inefficient propellers left the airship at the mercy of any strong wind, and by this time one of the engines had failed. After eighteen minutes in the air, with the weight mechanism jammed, starboard rudder out of action and one engine dead, the airship settled back on to the water. The trimming-weight and its supporting wire became entangled with a wooden stake in the water. The airship was impaled upon the stake, gas cells were damaged and the airship had to be cut free.

Repaired for a second flight, the airship flew for one-and-a-half hours. The flight came to a sudden end when a mechanic mistook distilled water for petrol and poured it into the fuel tank.

A third and final flight lasted twenty minutes. After it the airship was dismantled and the Count's airship company was liquidated.

«LZ2» A captive for the wind. It took Zeppelin five years to finance and build a second airship. Although her engines were five times more powerful than those of the previous airship she was too weak to fly against the wind. Her first and last flight was on 17 January 1906.

She rose suddenly off the water as far too much ballast was released. At about 1,500 feet the Count regained control by valving off hydrogen. The wind at this height was far stronger than it had been at ground level, and when the rudder jammed, the airship was carried north-east, rolling and pitching as she went. This violent movement flooded and starved the engines of fuel until the forward engine overheated and stopped. Soon afterwards the clutch of the other engine failed. They valved gas and then hit earth. The drag anchor was ripped off. Showing an amazing instinct and skill, Count Zeppelin and his crew brought the motorless airship back to the ground at Kisslegg, Allgau. She clipped the tops of two birch trees, then landed in swampy pasture. No one was hurt and the Zeppelin was only slightly damaged by the forced landing. She was staked out fore and aft on mooring posts and heavy weights but that night the wind played a return engagement. Had she been moored only at one end she would have swung before the wind. But she was captive, and by the time the handling crew arrived the airship was so badly smashed by cross-winds that the men from Friedrichshafen chopped her to pieces. Too late they realised that she could have been dismantled. Some parts – gondolas, shafts, propellers, valves and gears – were salvaged but most of the structure was fit only for the melting pot.

«LZ4» Miracle at Echterdingen. Without the LZ4 and its destruction, there would have been no 'miracle at Echterdingen' and the story of airships might have ended there. For in

LZ2: The mooring crew made a mistake.

1908, when the LZ4 created a world endurance record by a twelve-hour flight over Switzerland, there was no one building practical, rigid airships other than Count von Zeppelin.

On 4 August 1908, with a great deal of attention from the press, the LZ4 lifted away from her floating shed at Manzell on the Bodensee. She was attempting a twenty-four-hour flight.

Excited crowds watched her pass over Konstanz, Basel and Strasbourg, where she was below the height of the cathedral spire. All might have gone well but for a design fault that was a fundamental disadvantage for any craft trying for an endurance record: the engines were not connected to the main fuel supply. Each time the tank in the engine gondola was exhausted, more fuel had to be brought by hand along the dangerously cramped walkways.

It was about midday – after some six hours' flying – that the forward engine spluttered to a stop. The morning sun had been warming the hydrogen in the envelope, making the airship lighter and lighter. Now, deprived of half her power, the airship could no longer be controlled. While the refuelling continued, the airship rose higher and higher. At 2,700 feet, its 'pressure height', the automatic valves began to release the precious hydrogen to prevent the gas cells bursting.

The lost gas caused the airship to drop back towards the Rhine. Although by now the engine was turning, it was only by dropping ballast that the crew avoided a collision with a bridge.

An hour later, the after engine needed refuelling, and the whole business was repeated. Beyond Worms the airship ascended for a third time.

About four o'clock that afternoon the forward engine overheated after a fan belt snapped (the airships were so slow that they required fans to drive air through the engines' radiators). The airship continued northwards up the wide flat Rhine

valley at a speed no better than walking pace. All attempts to get the engine running again failed. At half-past five, after eleven hours in the air, the LZ4 became heavy, as the day cooled and the gas cooled too. She landed on a quiet bywater of the Rhine at Oppenheim, a few miles south of Mainz.

The fan belt was repaired. At ten-twenty that night she climbed back into the sky but the captain had to leave behind 1,550 lbs of equipment and two men.

Exactly as planned, the airship went to Mainz and turned round for the return journey. But now the wind along the Rhine valley that had helped the crew, was blowing in their face. And the engines gave trouble. First a fan-blade broke and then the forward engine overheated to a point where the bearing melted.

Now the LZ4 had only one engine, and when that needed refuelling, the airship became a motorless, free balloon. Near Stuttgart the airship suffered the indignity of being blown backwards. All through the night the crew tried to recognise the few lights of sleeping Rhineland towns and villages. At dawn the Count decided that he would bring the airship to earth somewhere near the Daimler works, and have the dud engine repaired or replaced.

It was 8 a.m. when they landed at Echterdingen (where Stuttgart airport stands today). Local villagers, soldiers and policemen all gave a hand for the mooring lines and the airship made a perfect landing.

The Daimler repair party were hard at work, and most of the crew eating lunch in the village, when the first sounds of thunder were heard. There were three men on board the moored airship; a mechanic on watch in the after gondola and two men refilling the water-ballast bags.

Soldiers had taken over as a mooring party. The gusts of wind that loosened the stakes tore the airship from the hands of the men at the rear of the craft. She lifted, with men still clinging to the ropes. They fell away. Seeing this, other soldiers at the front let go. The airship rose steeply into the sky.

Aboard the Zeppelin, the three men saw the ground racing past. The mechanic climbed along the bucking and rearing airship to open the gas valves from the forward gondola. The gas hissed and the nose of the airship dropped towards the ground. Driven before the wind, the airship was half a mile away before she landed again. She hit trees, ripping open the outer cover and some of the gas cells inside. To what extent spilled petrol contributed to the fire no one can be sure, but the three 'passengers' jumped and ran to safety before the gas exploded. Soon the LZ4 was no more than a tangle of hot metal and scorch marks in the grass.

Even newspapers that had not been covering the flight of the LZ4 splashed the story of its destruction. A 24-hour flight would have given the Zeppelin company government finance. Now the 70-year-old Count was penniless and depressed. But the disaster brought gifts of wine, hams, clothes, the contents of money-boxes, legacies and advice. Within one day, money equal to the cost of LZ4 had arrived.

Far left: Count von Zeppelin's airships always attracted a crowd and, by the time LZ4 flew, the old man was a popular celebrity. So the loss of this great airship saddened the whole of Germany.

Left: The tangled wreckage of LZ4.

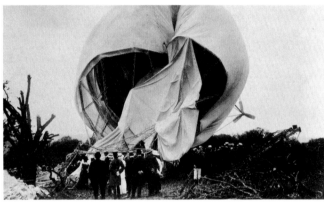

The Zeppelin Company was put on a sound financial footing with money enough to start subsidiary companies to make airship engines and airship sheds. More important was a company to make the fragile gas cells, for eventually it was discovered that the rubberised fabric used for the LZ4 cells could generate static electricity. This was possibly the cause of the fire.

«LZ5»

An airship in a pear tree. In 1909 the old man decided that he must train another airship pilot to take over from him. Dürr, his chief designer, was under instruction when the LZ5 attempted to fly non-stop to Berlin in May that year.

Dürr was at the elevator wheel – the most difficult and sensitive job on the airship. They flew on through the night. After the moon went down the night was pitch-black. Dürr brought the airship very low over a short line of lights.

The Count leaned over the side of the open gondola and bellowed, 'What place is this?'

'Schweinfurt railway station,' came the unsurprised reply.

After thirty-seven hours in the air, stiff with cold, tired from so long without sleep and short of fuel, even Count von Zeppelin admitted defeat. When daylight came he gave the order to land.

Dürr, on the elevator wheel, was flying the airship nose-down because she was light. The man on the rudder wheel could see nothing in front of him because the lowered nose of the airship obstructed his view. It was a comical misfortune that the airship should collide with a solitary pear tree on that flat, bare landscape.

The impact was enough to break the nose and deflate two front gas cells. Yet the LZ5 was about to prove that the wind did not always claim airships that were forced to land. Dürr, a taciturn young

Left top: After 38 hours in the air LZ5 made a forced landing in a field near Göppingen. It hit a solitary tree *(right and centre)*. The nose was damaged and the first two gas cells torn. The nose was repaired with poles from a nearby hop field *(left bottom)* and the airship was successfully flown home *(over page)*.

Swabian, had by this time had considerable design experience and was chief designer of this airship. He used poles from a hop field to lash together a new nose. A special train, from the airship base at Friedrichshafen, brought hydrogen. The forward engine was removed, together with as much other heavy equipment as could be spared. Then with a skeleton crew of five men, LZ5 flew home.

The story of LZ5 was not over. After being repaired she was purchased for the Army Airship Battalion at Cologne. But the Count got permission to demonstrate his airship at the International Aviation Exposition at Frankfurt-am-Main. The flight to Frankfurt, against fierce headwinds, was difficult enough, but the flight from there to Cologne was twice abandoned due to engine trouble and thunderstorms. The third attempt was successful and the LZ5 was renamed ZII and got an army crew.

It was not a popular acquisition. The army reported that her poor speed made her unsuitable for the wind conditions obtaining on half of the days of the average year.

The end of the airship came in April 1910 after a forced landing at Limburg. In spite of every effort to hold her down, she was wrenched from the hands of the military mooring party. With not a soul aboard, she soared into the air and then put her nose down and raced along the Lahn valley like a great white wraith. She hit a hillside near the railway line at Weilburg. The battered carcass crawled down the hill, tormented by the wind.

The crash of the LZ5 – ZII – came at the worst possible time for the Zeppelin Company's big expansion programme. The Count sent his right-hand man, Hugo Eckener, to the scene of the crash, where he tricked an army sergeant into saying the handling party had held the airship too loosely. It was a shabby trick and doubtful help for Zeppelin.

Left: The LZ5 was finally destroyed in 1910. After a forced landing, wind wrapped it round a hillside *(top)* and, as it rolled down the slope like a wounded monster *(lef centre and bottom)*, ripped its fabric cover away.

«MAYFLY»

His Majesty's Airship No. 1. In July 1908, alarmed by Count von Zeppelin's progress, the British navy ordered a rigid airship from Vickers at Barrow. Most of the design team were submarine experts. It was not ready until 1911. One of the delays was caused by a sailor who fell through the airship, damaging a gas cell. A longer delay came after it was discovered that the airship was far too heavy to fly. Its weight was partly due to such luxuries as Honduras mahogany woodwork and a ship's anchor.

The No. 1 airship was larger than any contemporary Zeppelin and the first airship to use an improved and strengthened metal alloy called duralumin. Perhaps this persuaded the men who were lightening the airship that she could manage without her keel. With some misgivings they removed it.

By 24 September 1911 the newly lightened airship was ready to test. She was being towed out of her waterside shed to a floating mast when a sudden wind tipped the vast airship on to her side. Slowly she righted herself. But, as she was turned to face out to the dock, there came the unmistakable sound of girders breaking. Far too long, and weakened by the removal of the keel, the No. 1 bent amidships, and then arched her back into the air.

Frightened by this, the men at the rear of the airship jumped overboard into the water. Lightened, the tail lifted. More girders broke, until the airship was almost in two parts, held together by sinews of twisted metal and fabric. Now the rear part of each half rose steeply off the water.

No one knew exactly how much damage had been done but, anxiously, Britain's only rigid airship was pushed back into her tight-fitting shed. This proved very difficult and the No. 1 was damaged beyond repair.

H.M. Airship No. 1 never flew, except to a height of three feet during the tests inside her shed. It was generally agreed that the sudden wind that hit her would have done similar damage to any airship of that time, and the Admiralty announced that no blame could be put upon the handling party. But Winston Churchill, the First Lord, prevented publication of the minutes, or even the findings, of the inquiry.

The disaster was used to settle all kinds of vendettas among the Admirals. The rigid airship programme was not continued and the No. 1, now popularly called the *Mayfly*, was left to rot in the hangar at Barrow, while the government argued with Vickers about who owned the wreck.

Left: The *Mayfly* was originally designed with a strong keel as seen in this photograph. Later the keel was removed. The redesigned airship was too weak and broke in half *(right)* as it was taken out of its waterside shed *(over page)*.

15

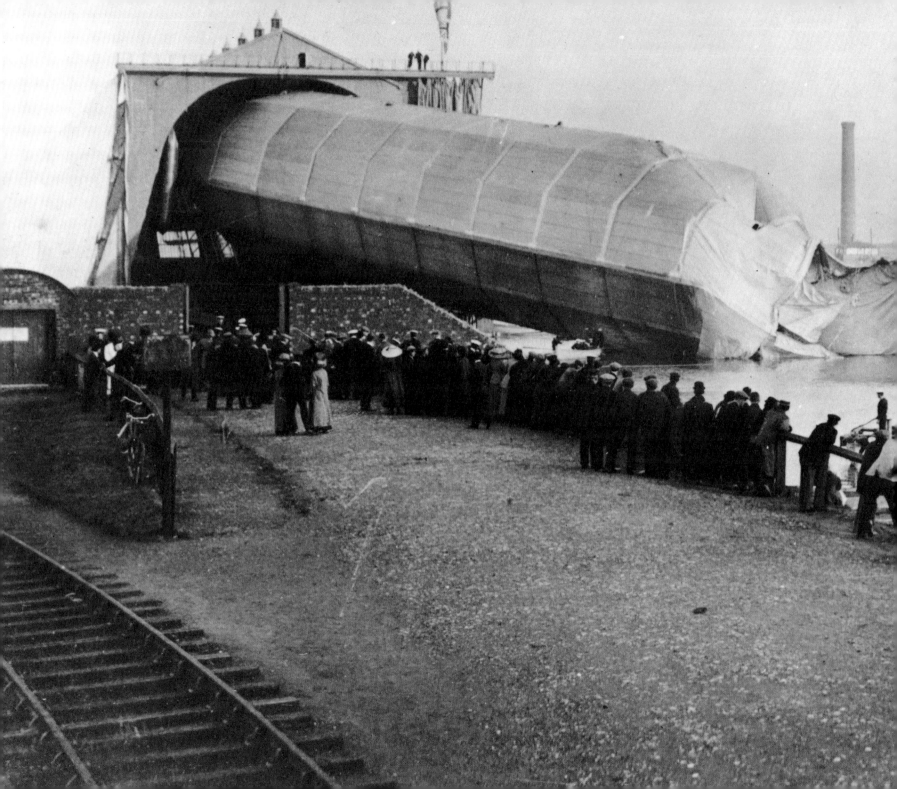

«LZ6» AND «LZ7 DEUTSCHLAND»

Zeppelin and Dürr, his chief designer, were learning a great deal about the design of airships. And they were learning a great deal about operating them, too. Some of the lessons were bitter ones.

The LZ7, *Deutschland*, suffered engine failure and crashed into the Teutoburg Forest just nine days after the test flight.

The LZ6, hurriedly lengthened to replace *Deutschland*, thereby became the first passenger-carrying rigid airship. But after only a few weeks she was destroyed, when a careless mechanic, using petrol as a cleaning fluid, caused a fire. Another mechanic threw more petrol on the flames, believing it was water.

«LZ8 ERSATZ DEUTSCHLAND»

The next airship, the LZ8, *Ersatz Deutschland*, also had a short life. Passengers were inside her as she was walked out of her hangar at Düsseldorf into a brisk cross-wind. Hugo Eckener was depending on the big wind shelters for protection, but as the airship came past the end of them the wind seized her.

Snatched from the hands of the 300-strong mooring crew, the airship's tail was impaled upon the screens while her nose was propped high on the shed roof. The terrified passengers had to be rescued using fire ladders.

«LZ10 SCHWÄBEN»

Between 1910 and the outbreak of war in 1914 the

Top left: LZ8, *Ersatz Deutschland*, was snatched up by a gust of wind so that its nose was propped on top of its hangar. As it crashed to earth the rear part of the frame was impaled upon the huge wind shelters **(centre left)**. From the tilted passenger compartment rescues were made by fire escape **(right)**. Finally the whole shattered airship toppled to the ground **(bottom left)**.

Zeppelin operating company DELAG lost four airships: *Deutschland I* and *II*, *Schwäben* and the LZ6. But none was destroyed in the air, and no loss was due to structural failure or design faults. And not one passenger was killed or even injured.

But the first Zeppelin fatalities had already occurred, and the victims were sailors.

‹‹L1›› The first fatalities.

The German navy's first rigid airship (works number LZ14) was scouting for the High Seas Fleet on 9 September 1913 sixteen miles off the coast of Heligoland. Weather reporting was still primitive and weather forecasting even more so – understanding of the turbulent air that accompanies the progress of a cold front, negligible.

The light cruiser SMS *Köln*, far to the west of the airship, sent a radio message warning of a line-squall. When the officers of L1 received it they probably had little idea of its dangers.

The violent wind that brought the airship down almost upon the waves was just as unexpected as the updraught that took her up beyond 'pressure height' and emptied the hydrogen from her. She fell back towards the ocean as the crew emptied the ballast, slipped the fuel tanks and threw all movable weight overboard, but she went head-first into the

stormy ocean and broke up.

These early airships had open, boat-like gondolas. The tangled metal and fabric and wires fell upon the men and trapped them there as she sank. Six men were rescued from the water; fourteen died. These were the first Zeppelin fatalities. It was peace-time and all Germany mourned.

‹‹L2›› Exactly what the customer wanted.

The German navy had opinions about airship design. Their second rigid was exactly what they specified. Limited by the dimensions of their shed, the navy wanted as much airship as the shed would take. By bringing the gondolas much closer to the envelope, they could get a much larger airship into the shed. And the envelope could be even larger if the keel – taking up so much space between cars and gas bags – could be inside the rings of the structure instead of under them.

The Count didn't like outside interference, especially when he was forced to agree to it. However, the finished airship looked good. Grudgingly the Count congratulated the navy.

There were other changes too. Count von Zeppelin had always insisted that a pilot needed the feel of the wind on his face but the navy fitted celluloid windscreens to the engine gondolas. These screens were so large that they touched the bottom of the envelope. All was set for disaster.

On 17 October 1913, just five weeks after the L1 crash, L2 was preparing for her altitude test. A delay in starting one of the engines kept her in the sun while her hydrogen warmed. Once aloft she rose fast and went up to 'pressure height' where gas was valved from the bases of the gas cells.

The released gas floated through the enclosed keel, mixing with just enough air to make an explosive mixture. To carry it down from the keel to the hot parts of the engine, there was the vacuum

The crew of the Zeppelin *Schwäben* have a group photograph taken to commemorate the 100th flight of the airship.

Left: Boats at the floating wreckage of L1 the German Naval Zeppelin No. 1.

Right: L2, the second rigid airship of the German Navy, exploded in mid-air.

being created behind the new-style windscreens.

The gas mixture exploded like a bomb and ignited the gas cells one by one as the airship fell. Before the blazing wreckage hit the ground the flames had found another gas-air mixture and the airship exploded again, scattering melting alloy until the remains hit the ground with a cannonade of exploding fuel tanks. No one could get near the wreckage. Three badly burned men crawled out of her alive but none survived the night.

Forgetting the congratulations he had offered the designer, now dead in the crash, von Zeppelin publicly blamed the navy for the disaster. At the funeral for the victims the old Count sought out Grossadmiral von Tirpitz and argued bitterly.

«ZIX»

The German army went to war believing that the Zeppelin provided the ground forces with an entirely new sort of reconnaissance force. Army airships equipped with air cameras and even photographic darkrooms went to war as an élite force. But within a few weeks its hopes were shattered.

At first the airship crews laughed to see ragged Russian infantry firing at them with ancient rifles, but the laughter was short-lived. These enormous targets, that could seldom get above 6,000 feet, provided even the rawest recruit with a chance to score a hit on the gas bags. Time after time the leaking airships were forced to turn back and head for home. Sometimes they failed to make it.

Four of the army's six Zeppelins were lost in the first month of fighting. And in the west the Germans found that the airship bases were vulnerable to sneak bombing attacks such as the one that destroyed the ZIX (LZ25) in her Düsseldorf shed on 8 October 1914.

In Germany the men who had staked their military careers upon the airship were anxious to find a new role for them. They had not far to look. For many years thrillers and comics had been offering the public stories about airships bombing the capital cities of Europe. This, decided the airship chiefs, must be the answer. So strategic bombing was invented.

«L3»

First over England! Captain Hans Fritz took L3 and a crew of fifteen and found Yarmouth using parachute flares on a dark rainy night in January 1915. It was a remarkable feat of navigation and, although the bombs had little effect upon the course of the war, it was the beginning of a new fighting role for the airship.

But L3's days were numbered. In the failing light of an afternoon in February of that same winter she was heading for Germany in the face of gale-force south winds. They had been scouting along the Norwegian coastline to see if the route was clear of British warships before a steamer went that way to German East Africa. One engine had failed soon after take-off. Now a second one stopped and the men realised that they would never get their airship home, even to the destroyers that were ordered to meet them at sea.

The captain brought her down on Fanö Island, Denmark, without injuring anyone. But the impact bent the whole framework. Hans Fritz destroyed his codebooks and then set fire to his airship. There could be no escape from the island and the Germans were all interned. But the wreckage was something of a sensation and people came from far and wide to see the awesome flying machine.

«SL5»

Zeppelin's only serious rival. Dr Johann Schütte, of Danzig University, became Count Zeppelin's only serious rival in the field of rigid-airship construction. Schütte invented many novel and successful ideas that

Right: The wreck of L2.

Over page: People of the island of Fanö came to see the remains of L3.

shaped the next generation of airships, notably the simple tailplane design, enclosed control car and the way in which propellers were coupled directly to the engines. However, the German navy was prejudiced against Schütte-Lanz airships, complaining that the laminated plywood (which Schütte used in place of metal) was not suited to flights over water. Additionally, Grossadmiral von Tirpitz, who decided such matters, strongly disliked Schütte.

Whatever was the truth of the navy's complaints, these fragile machines were not well suited to the wear and tear that wartime flying imposed upon them.

On the eastern front conditions were harsh for airships even in summer. In July 1915 the fifth Schütte-Lanz airship force-landed after suffering severe damage in a gale that continued to torment the structure until it was a total wreck.

«L6»

Where are we? The airship crews were learning many new sciences. Baron von Buttlar Brandenfels received a sharp lesson about barometric pressure while commanding the L6 in February 1915. This was one of the M class, a pre-war design and small by German standards, but still 518 feet long and 50 feet in diameter.

They were searching the North Sea coast for a missing seaplane, and as it grew dark the wind increased to gale force. They crossed the desolate region at the mouth of the Weser and returned to their base at Nordholz. There a searchlight shone into their faces, apparently signalling them away.

Blinded, the airship-men saw a hangar roof and a gasometer passing very close as they tried to gain height. Suddenly there was a loud crash. Von Buttlar looked at the altimeter. It read 100 metres. He signalled to stop the stern engines and leaned out of the car to shout, 'Where are we?' into the darkness.

'In a wood,' came the answer.

I knew that voice, said von Buttlar. It was one of my petty officers.

'Man alive,' shouted the captain (or words to that effect). 'How did you get there?'

'Fell out of the after car, sir,' said the petty officer, who had fallen on to a roof and slid down it to a dung heap.

The L6 was jammed tight on to a pine wood. With the wind in his face and only the front hundred feet of the airship impaled on the trees, von Buttlar sent all the crew down to the ground, except for his elevator man. Lightened, the airship rose off the trees, while the headwind pushed her back until she was clear of the wood.

Von Buttlar then mobilised men, women and children from the village to help manhandle the airship along the road back to the base. Everyone enjoyed it, none more than the sailors who were appointed to chopping down telegraph poles. Before the night was over, the L6 was back in her shed, and von Buttlar had realised that in thunderstorms barometers no longer provide a reliable way to measure height. The failure of the radio generator had prevented him from getting the standard barometer check. L6 ended her life in a hangar fire, an accident during the inflation process.

Of the new sciences, navigation proved the trickiest to master. In April 1915, after a raid over England with the L6, von Buttlar and his watch officer, von Schiller (later to command the *Graf Zeppelin*), were in a Hamburg restaurant trying to complete their raid report. Then, into the bar came a newspaper seller. He offered them a special edition that headlined their raid with L6 as an attack on Maldon, England. The report had been filed by the London correspondent of a Rotterdam paper. We

Baron von Buttlar (seated), captain of L6, and his watch officer, von Schiller, later to command the *Graf Zeppelin*.

Left: Violent winds damaged SL5 in flight. Deflated gas cells caused the rear part of the structure to collapse while the nose remained in the air.

put Maldon on the report, said von Buttlar, and two weeks later I was commended for my accurate navigation.

The airship bases developed special techniques for bringing in crippled airships. At Nordholz they put five captive balloons up through fog or ground mist. Each balloon was manned, with signalling lights and a telephone link to the ground.

Every available man was summoned out for an emergency landing. Four hundred men to an airship was the rule. At the approach of an airship in difficulties the sirens would sound and the 'ground acrobats' – a reference to the way the mooring crew were so often thrown off their feet by the tugs of the ropes – were instructed to shout, clap, cheer and whistle as soon as they saw the shape of the airship emerging through the fog. This warned the Zeppelin crew that they were near the ground.

This sort of greeting sometimes frightened the airship-men into thinking they were about to crash. Then the poor 'ground acrobats' received a few tons of water ballast (liberally spiked with foul-smelling anti-freeze). More drastically, fuel tanks and loose equipment were dropped as the airship shed weight.

Sometimes the airships could not get back to base and had to land in open country without a mooring crew; an extremely difficult feat. And it was not very unusual for a force-landed airship to be walked across country, as von Buttlar's L6 had been. On at least one occasion, a mooring party from Nordholz walked an airship 5 kilometres across country, following their brass band.

Even in high summer the crews suffered from the cold on trips that lasted anything up to twenty-four hours. At the start of the war the gondolas were open to wind and rain. Even when this was rectified the greater heights to which the airships were forced meant worse suffering. The physical dangers of oxygen-deprivation were little understood at the time, and oxygen was not used until the airships were very high, and it consisted only of oxygen bottles and rubber tubes. Men moving about had to manage without oxygen until they reached the next supply point. Apart from some self-warming canned food there was no heat on the airship. In the control car, the *Steuermann* (helmsman) sometimes carried a hip-flask of schnapps. On the C.O.'s orders a tot could be issued when the airship went over 4,000 metres but some commanders insisted on a 'dry' ship however cold it was.

‹‹LZ38›› Bombed in its shed. On the night of 6 June 1915, the German

Far left: The nose of von Buttlar's airship after the forced landing in a pine wood.

Left: The crew of LZ38 the first airship to attack London. Soon afterwards the Zeppelin was destroyed in its shed by a bombing attack *(right)*.

army and navy for the first time concerted their attacks on England. The army contributed three Zeppelins to the attack. One of them was the first of a new generation of airships, the P class. This LZ38 was only 7 weeks old but her massive 1,126,400 cubic feet – and top speed of 56 m.p.h. – had already convinced both army and navy experts that this should be the standard war-time design. Sheds were tailored to suit such giants.

That night the LZ38 did not get to England. She returned to her base after having engine trouble. She was in her shed at Evere, near Brussels, at dawn when two British aircraft made a bombing attack, using tiny 20-lb bombs. They were enough; the LZ38's million cubic feet of gas ignited and the flames reached far into the sky.

«LZ37» Shot down by aeroplane. The bombers were from Britain's Naval Squadron No. 1 sent to Dunkirk with orders to search for German airships. Another member of the Squadron was in the air that night. He sighted LZ37 over Ostend and gave chase, overtaking the airship near Bruges.

The LZ37 was a small pre-war design, built in the shed at Potsdam, Berlin. It was to be the first Zeppelin brought down by an aeroplane.

Ordinary bullets were seldom fatal for airships. If fired from underneath, there was not much chance that they would ignite the gas. Unless they went out through the upper side the lighter-than-air gas did not even leak. But aeroplanes *above* the airships were a greater danger. In this case the pilot of the aeroplane actually bombed LZ37 in flight. This is the pilot's report.

Sir, I have the honour to report as follows: I left Furnes at 1.0 am on June 7th on Morane No. 3253 under orders to proceed to look for Zeppelins and attack the Berchem Ste. Agathe airship shed with six 20-lb bombs. On arriving at Dixmude at 1.05 am I observed a Zeppelin apparently over Ostend and proceeded in chase of same. I arrived at close quarters a few miles past Bruges at 1.50 am and the airship opened heavy maxim fire, so I retreated to gain height and the airship turned and followed me. At 2.15 he seemed to stop firing and at 2.25 am I came behind, but well above the Zeppelin; height then 11,000 feet, and then switched off my engine to descend on top of him. When close above him, at 7,000 feet I dropped my bombs, and, whilst releasing the last, there was an explosion which lifted my machine and turned it over. The aeroplane was out of control for a short period, but went into a nose dive, and the control was gained.

I then saw that the Zeppelin was on the ground in flames and also that there were pieces of something burning in the air all the way down.

The joint on my petrol pipe and pump from the back tank was broken, and at about 2.40 am I was forced to land and repair my pump.

I landed at the back of a forest close to a farmhouse; the district is unknown on account of the fog and the continuous changing of course. I made preparations to set the machine on fire but apparently was not observed, so was enabled to effect a repair, and continued at 3.15 am in a south westerly direction after

The gravestone of Flt Sub-Lieutenant Warneford V.C. who dropped a bomb on LZ37 and destroyed it in flight.

considerable difficulty in starting my engine single handed.

I tried several times to find my whereabouts by descending through the clouds, but was unable to do so. So eventually I landed and found out that I was at Cape Gris-Nez, and took in some petrol. When the weather cleared I was able to proceed and arrived at the aerodrome about 10.30 am. As far as could be seen the colour of the airship was green on top and yellow below and there was no machine or gun platform on top.

I have the honour to be, Sir, Your obedient servant,
R. A. J. Warneford. Flt. Sub-Lieutenant.

Some of the crew of the blazing LZ37 jumped to their deaths. Alone in the control car the helmsman threw himself flat on the floor as the fire roasted him. Then the whole control car fell off its mounting and crashed through the roof of a convent. The helmsman was thrown out and landed unconscious in a bed. He was the only survivor.

King George V immediately awarded the Victoria Cross to Warneford, but the young flyer enjoyed only a few days of glory. Flying out of Paris in a new plane, with the Legion of Honour on his chest and an American reporter in the passenger seat, he crashed. Both men died. Press stories said the medal had pierced Warneford's heart.

For the Army Airship Service, the night had proved too tragic. The last two army airships were transferred from Belgium to the Russian front.

«L12» **Sailing into harbour.** Now the Naval Airship Division pressed the Kaiser for permission to attack London. He agreed, and on the afternoon of 9 August 1915 five airships were sitting on the horizon, waiting for darkness to descend upon the capital.

None of the airships found London; darkness,

poor navigation, thunderstorms and the weight of rain-water all militated against the raiders.

The L12, one of the navy's million-cubic-feet P type Zeppelins, dropped her bombs in the sea near Dover, although the captain thought he was over Harwich fifty miles away. A three-inch anti-aircraft gun fired ten rounds at the airship and the gunners said they saw smoke but this was probably the spray of water ballast falling from the airship as she climbed up out of range.

As the L12 turned back, the riggers were already reporting that two aft gas cells were holed and leaking badly. The captain set a course for the Belgian coast and ordered the sagging tail to be brought up. As the airship limped home the gas loss forced the elevator man to turn the wheel until the airship was at the full descent position; but still she dropped tail-heavy towards the sea.

They dumped water ballast, and fuel tanks, and everything they could wrench loose from the doomed ship but at 3.40, in that dark hour before dawn, she hit the sea. There was still a lot of gas in the cells and the wind caught her. A mechanic thrown out of the airship had to swim strenuously for an hour to get back aboard the floating wreckage.

When daylight came, a German torpedo boat found them. At the airship captain's request, the wreckage was towed to Ostend, but during the journey six aircraft of the R.N. Squadron from Dunkirk unsuccessfully bombed them. Tugs brought the airship to the quayside, where a crane was used to salvage the gondolas. Some hydrogen caught fire as the bow was being craned up and it is doubtful whether its value outweighed the time and trouble spent on it.

‹‹L10›› Struck by lightning.

In thunderstorms the crews feared lightning more than turbulence. One handbook of 1910 described the prospect of aerial electricity as 'one of the most serious risks the airship will be subjected to'. Certainly the stories about St Elmo's fire (the static electricity visible sometimes in thunderstorms) did nothing to allay such fears. There were accounts, undoubtedly true ones, of the blue flickering lights being seen on all parts of the airships. One crew had worn haloes of electricity, due to the wire rings in their naval hats.

Several airships were struck by lightning. The LZ98 had a melted metal support to mark the place. But the only recorded destruction of an airship by lightning was on 3 September 1915, as the L10 was coming home over the North Sea. In full view of the officers and men on the landing field, the airship climbed to valve off gas before landing – a necessity due to the warm sunshine, which had made the airship light.

The watchers on the ground felt a movement of air and recognised the signs of a thunderstorm. As the L10 disappeared for a moment behind darkening cloud, the sky went red. The airship dropped out of the cloud, burning from end to end, and slightly nose-down. She dropped into the shallow waters at the mouth of the River Elbe and the flames turned to smoke. All nineteen crewmen died.

Her recording barograph was recovered, and the inquiry ordered that in the future airships must not go to 'pressure height' in the vicinity of thunderstorms. The release of gas into the surrounding air produced an explosive mixture.

‹‹L15›› Sunk in the Thames Estuary.

On 31 March 1916 came the first of a series of raids during which the Zeppelins raided England every day. There were seven airships on this attack. The night was very dark but by good luck or great skill a searchlight found L15 as she cruised at 7,500 feet over London, following the

Opposite: British gunfire damaged L12. It fell into the sea near Dover and was towed to Ostend by a German boat *(centre)*, but caught fire as it was being lifted *(bottom)* on to the quay.

shiny course of the river. Two more searchlights turned on to her and now, blinded by the beams, the men in the control car knew that they had little chance of getting home.

The anti-aircraft guns fired. Shrapnel from one shell hit the L15 amidships, holing five gas cells. The airship dropped, turning as she went. The guns stopped firing. It was an ominous silence that usually meant the fighter planes were up. This was confirmed when the dark, creaking structure echoed with the sound of the machine gun that was mounted on the upper side of the airship's envelope.

The crew discharged ballast, guns, code books and even the wireless, but the airship was deflating rapidly and the girder work weakened to a point of collapse. Two of the gas cells emptied, and, weakened at these two places, the airship folded up and fell into the Thames Estuary.

The crew shed their fur coats, sheepskin gloves and boots and jumped into the water. Six armed trawlers found them and one opened fire but stopped when an RN destroyer arrived. Seventeen crewmen were made prisoner, one drowned. The last men off the floating wreck slashed the gas cells. The L15 was taken in tow but did not reach land.

《L19》 Messages in a bottle. Worse was the fate of L19, returning from a raid over England on 1 February 1916. This P class airship had three of her four engines fail, and drifted over neutral Holland. Although the airship was obviously out of control, the Dutch fired on her. Holed, the L19 was blown out over the fog of the North Sea until she came down in the water.

The crew climbed up on the floating remains of the airship, and huddled together for warmth. A Reuter's message said an English fishing boat had reported seeing the wreckage but was unable to rescue the crew.

Nothing else was heard about the L19 until bottles containing messages from the crew were washed up on to the Norwegian coast. One was a formal report from the airship captain. Another, from one of the officers, said, 'Two days and two nights afloat. No help. Bless you. An English fishing steamer wouldn't rescue us. Erwin.'

Another message said, 'My dear Ada and Mother. It is eleven in the morning, February second. This morning a fishing steamer, an English one, passed by but refused to rescue us. It was the King Stephen out of Grimsby. Courage failing; storm coming up. Still thinking of you. Hans. At eleven-thirty we prayed and said farewell to each other. Your Hans.'

《L20》 Shipwrecked mariners. On 2 May 1916 eight airships set out to bomb Scotland. The L20 encountered a whole catalogue of appalling weather: winds, cloud, rain, fog and snow. The ice prevented the navigator getting position checks and when daylight came they were near the Orkney Islands. They realised that there could be no hope of getting back to Germany, for there wasn't enough fuel aboard. In the face of south-east winds up to 40 m.p.h. they

An artist's impression from the *Illustrated London News* shows the trawler *King Stephen* which refused to pick up survivors from the sinking wreck of L19. Another reconstruction showing the plight of the crew appears on the title page of this book.

Left: L15, its back broken, floats in the Thames Estuary.

had to give up the idea of even getting to a rendezvous with German naval units off Denmark. Desperately they turned for Norway.

The turbulence from the Norwegian mountains made the airship difficult to control. Conscious of the non-swimmers aboard the captain brought her down in a fiord. The impact did considerable damage and as eight men jumped overboard the airship rose up over the 150-feet-high cliffs, tearing the after gondola off as it scraped across the pinnacle, and more of the crew were thrown out across the forbidding landscape.

The rest of the crew cut the gas cells. Back broken, the airship fell back into the sea again. There some of the crew were rescued by a fishing boat, and as shipwrecked mariners were returned to Germany. The rest of the crew on land were treated as military personnel and interned.

‹‹L22›› A nose in the doorway.
Having returned from a reconnaissance flight, the L22 landed at Tondern, very near the Danish border, before noon on 17 April 1916. The wind was strong enough, and gusty enough, to make the airship difficult to handle on the ground. All that afternoon there were attempts to put this new airship into the vast double shed that was

code-named 'Toska'. Already the L18 had burned in this shed the previous November and before the end of the year the L24 would break across the doors and burn to take L17 up in flames with her.

Late that afternoon they ceased trying and waited until evening before making another attempt. It was nearly midnight then, with the wind no more than about 10 m.p.h. Then one of the railway trolleys that carried the airship into the shed broke. When the port trolley went, the bow swung starboard and struck the frame of the huge doors. So fragile were the great ships that 160 feet of the airship structure was broken. Men came from the Zeppelin factory at Friedrichshafen to do the repairs.

The wrecked airship was pulled right into the hangar lest the wind continue the destruction. The photo was taken the next day. The rather elegantly shaped design on the upper part of the damaged nose is the machine gunner's position and gun-mounting.

‹‹L33››
In September 1916 the German naval Zeppelin L33 raided England. It ran the gauntlet of accurate gunfire before being attacked by an aeroplane. The airship was already sinking towards the ground as it passed over the coast near West Mersea. Rather than go into the

Left: L20 hit the ground in Norway and then fell into the sea.

Right: L22 after the accident.

33

sea, the captain turned back and force-landed in a field near Little Wigborough, Essex, only 20 yards from a cottage. The captain knocked on the door to warn the residents that he was going to set the wreck ablaze. Seeing the enormous wreckage towering over them, the family inside hid in a cupboard and did not answer. In the event there was hardly enough hydrogen left to catch fire. The captain marched his crew up the lane until they met a special constable on his bicycle. 'You come along with me,' said the policeman and led the parade to Peldon Post Office and arrested them.

≪L48≫ Vulnerable at 13,000 feet.

The crews of badly holed airships stood a good chance of survival, even if descent was into water. Fire was often fatal for all aboard. The few who escaped from blazing airships were usually at an altitude just enough to burn off the hydrogen by the time they hit the ground. The L48, shot down by aircraft over Theberton, Suffolk, was less than a month old when she burned. The crew were on their thirteenth bombing mission. Her frozen compass might have been the reason for coming down to 13,000 feet or it might have been the trouble the crew were having with two of the engines. When the fighters found her she was heading north and the night was so clear that the guns and searchlights were already engaged.

At this stage of the war, 17 June 1917, no guns and no fighters – and few searchlights either – could reach the height climbers at their maximum altitude, but here at 13,500 feet the gas cells were punctured by drum after drum of machine-gun fire. Inside the envelope, one crewman saw streams of tracer going right through her, and he climbed up the girders. The flames started at the tail and ran forward along both sides. As the gas burned away she fell in a near horizontal attitude. Because she remained level, she fell very slowly, taking an estimated five minutes to hit the ground.

In the control car, the captain removed his leather coat and overalls, certain they were dropping on to water. Another officer, in the forward gondola, was seen to grip the edge of the map table as screams came from men in the blazing tail section.

The tail section hit the ground first. The only survivors – three of them – were placed well forward. The heavy flying clothes protected them to some extent, and one man emerged with a charred fur coat. One of the survivors was so badly injured that he died, on Armistice Day 1918. Of the other two, one insists that a radio message from Germany promised them tail winds at 13,000 feet.

≪L38≫ Target: St Petersburg.

The idea of bombing the Russian capital had been discussed since the start of the war. It was a long journey for the earlier types of Zeppelin but by December 1916, larger airships and long winter nights persuaded the German navy to position L38 at Wainoden, Courland, from which it was a 400-mile journey to the target.

The airship-men now had to contend with the terrible weather that winter brings to northern Russia. Caution prevailed and they were assigned

34 Guarding L48.

Right: The enormous wreckage of L33 frightened the family in the cottage.

to other targets. The crews endured misery from cold so cruel that it congealed the lubricant, and froze the compass and even the radiator of a briefly stopped engine.

Snow weighed the airship and chunks of ice flew from the propellor blades and pierced the fragile gas cells. Blinded by falling snow and only just under control, L38 force-landed in German-occupied Russia. Before there was time to moor it down, the wind had fractured the framework and made it a complete wreck. In the photograph of the overturned airship, the bomb-doors can be seen along the airship's underside.

«L55» The height climber.

The 'height climber' was a new sort of airship that came into action in August 1917 specially to elude the British defences. These rather fragile machines were of the enormous L30 type; 645 feet long, they had a gas capacity of about 2 million cubic feet. But the designers had lightened the structure and there were 5 engines instead of 6.

A few minutes after noon on 19 October 1917, L55 left her base at Ahlhorn and joined ten other naval airships heading towards England (two others were to have flown but cross-winds prevented them leaving the hangars). It was a long, slow journey to position the airships so that they could bomb England under cover of darkness.

L55 bombed Hitchin and Hatfield but thought they were bombing Birmingham. On the way home no less than three engines failed, leaving only two to help the giant airship fight the fierce winds. She crossed the western front near Rheims (height climbers had no need to avoid the firing line) but sighted two aircraft. By this time, the use of incendiary and explosive bullets had made the aeroplane a fearful enemy. The L55 put up its nose and eventually reached the astounding height of 7,500

metres – about five miles. It remains the altitude record for any airship.

The helmsman collapsed and the thermometer registered 35 degrees below zero. The engines starved of oxygen and the crew became sluggish in thought and action. She would undoubtedly have gone on until her valves opened and she fell back to earth like a stone, had not the watch officer gone through the airship coaxing the crew forward by giving them chocolate (one of the only foods that remained edible in freezing temperatures). The weight of the men righted the ship, and she came back under control but continued to tilt alarmingly, sometimes as much as 45 degrees.

Heavy rain and cloud made visibility poor and even when they came as low as they dared the navigator mistook Darmstadt for Aachen, about 125 miles away. The shortage of fuel and the coming of darkness made the commander anxious to put his ship down upon the earth. At one point the radio antenna was torn off as they passed low over a wood. Finally the airship hit the ground very heavily. It was in a forest clearing near Tiefenort on the river Werra. They were 200 miles from home and it was clear from the crippled structure and smashed gondolas that their airship would never fly again. They began to dismantle the wreck.

The L55's altitude record was made while returning from 'the silent raid', the last big raid of the war. There were high-altitude winds that night, unsuspected by the forecasters, and the airships were scattered across Europe. One captain reported that he had made a remarkable journey 'from Denmark to the Riviera by way of London and Paris in twenty hours'.

«L49» Captured intact.

Of the airships that set out that night, five did not return. One of these was L49, a modified height

Right: L38. The plan to bomb St Petersburg ended in disaster.

climber, although like all the other airships she had not yet been fitted with engines suitable for use in the thin upper air.

The L49's English landfall was 100 miles in error and its bombs fell in open country. Three of her engines failed, due probably to oxygen lack and the effect it had on the crew. Only a few weeks previously L49's elevator man had dropped dead during an altitude flight.

Blown across France by the unexpected winds, they were close behind L44 as the French guns shot that airship down in flames. Lost and demoralised, the L49 turned back west in the belief they were near Holland. At 6,500 feet they were jumped by French fighter planes which riddled them with bullets but, lacking incendiary ammunition, could not set them ablaze.

Frozen and exhausted, unable to recognise the ground, they hit the trees near Bourbonne-les-Bains, France. They tried to set light to the airship but failed. The crew were taken prisoner (the executive officer, K. O. Dehn, later became a permanent resident in London, where he died in 1975).

Delighted with having a height climber captured almost intact, the Allied experts made detailed plans of the ship and it became the basis for British airship designs and also for the American airship *Shenandoah*.

«L46 – L47 – L51 – L58 SL20»
Disaster at Ahlhorn. The danger of fire was not lessened when the airship landed. The presence of oil and petrol (the latter often used for cleaning), the heat and sparks of the early engines, gas cells that could never be completely leak-proof, all contributed to the many disasters. Inflating gas bags was particularly hazardous. At Ahlhorn, on 5 January 1918, a sudden roar of flame from the after gondola of L51 totally destroyed five airships, four of them were the 2-million-cubic-foot Zeppelins and the other a similarly gigantic Schütte-Lanz airship. Roaring along the gas lines from shed to shed, the fire reached across the long spaces between them. It burned out two of the giant double-hangars, and severely damaged two others. It was the worst blow the airship service had ever suffered. Some spoke of sabotage. This was unlikely but the precise cause was never discovered.

By early 1917, the airship was fighting a losing battle against the aeroplane, not only in the skies of England and France but in German factories too, where the airship's allocation of vital materials such as aluminium and rubber was cut drastically.

The army airships had been despatched upon an ambitious series of raids: against St Petersburg (Leningrad), Bucharest, the Ploesti oil fields, Black Sea bases, the Greek islands and the naval base at Taranto in the toe of Italy. Partly due to the weather in the first months of 1917, the results were so disappointing that the army disbanded its airship service altogether. Apart from two R class 2-million-cubic-feet ships which were handed over to the navy, its airships – thirteen in all – were dismantled and their crews assigned to other duties.

Left: One of the huge airship hangars at the German naval airship base at Ahlhorn was gutted by fire.

«L70» Strasser dies.

But Fregatten-kapitän Strasser, chief of the naval airships, did not give up so easily. He took his R class ships and lightened them drastically, ordering that future airships should have a simplified structure. These new airships had to be flown with great care and skill in the dense air of low altitudes, but they were able to get as high as 20,000 feet to bomb. Encouraged by this, Strasser persuaded the Zeppelin factory to give him 'the final type'. It had an extra gas cell of 200,000 cubic feet, and could take 6,600 lbs of bombs up to 23,000 feet. No fighter plane could get up to this height, and no gun could get anywhere near it.

This new immunity from attack gave the Zeppelin commanders false confidence about the ability of the defences. The L70, the first of the new 'final type' X class ships, was leading a formation of three when she came in sight of the English coast at dusk on 5 August 1918. This raid was commanded by the 'leader of airships' in person. Keeping with his other airships, Peter Strasser's altitude was no more than 16,500 feet. And this was within the capability of certain British aircraft.

A DH4 climbed over the sea to intercept the formation. This lone aeroplane made a head-on attack on L70, passing underneath and slightly to one side, to avoid the trailing radio antenna. The gunner was firing explosive bullets, concentrating his fire on one spot. Flames began near the tail, which dropped until the airship was almost vertical, hanging in the air by the power of her seven screaming engines. Only then, blazing from end to end, did the airship begin to fall towards the sea.

In the gathering darkness, other British aviators far below and still climbing were awestruck by the disintegrating tangle of gaseous flames that fell past them through the cloud layers, to make great pools of yellow sky.

«L53» Victim of an experiment.

For the airship service, the death of Peter Strasser came as a terrible blow. The men of L53 watched the L70 burn and began to climb above the clouds. Bombs were dropped, but their airship was still over the sea.

But for the L53, too, a fiery death was close at hand. Only a few days later it was on a routine patrol near the Dutch coast when, from a height of 19,000 feet, British naval forces were sighted making smoke screens. L53 went for a closer look, confident in the knowledge that it was far beyond the range of any Allied airfield.

The ships were part of a British trap, and the L53 was flying into it. Nearby, a RN Camel fighter was sitting on a floating platform towed behind a destroyer. By means of high-speed tow into the wind, it was just possible for the Camel to get airborne. With considerable difficulty, slipping and sliding in the thin upper air, the pilot reached 18,000 feet. He took another half-an-hour to reach 18,700 feet, from which he fired at the Zeppelin above him. Again the horrifying effect of the indendiary and explosive bullets was demonstrated. The L53 caught fire and dived head-first, breaking up as it fell into the sea. For the airship-men the war had become a fiery nightmare, and survivors were rare.

Fregattenkapitän Peter Strasser. His skill and determination was the driving force of the German airship service. He died in L70.

Left: A British naval biplane takes off from a platform towed by a destroyer. By this device L53 was shot down.

«L54»«L60»

Carrier strike. In July 1918, the Royal Navy had proved – for the first time in history – the effectiveness of the aircraft carrier. HMS *Furious* launched seven Camels to bomb the airship base at Tondern near the Danish border. L54 and L60 were destroyed,

Landings on HMS *Furious* proved hazardous, as this photo shows, and so the Camels ditched or went to neutral Denmark.

Visible in the air and on the ground, vulnerable to aircraft and to weather, the airship was no longer an effective war weapon. But as an engineering achievement, the airship was an astounding success. Of all the rigid airships manufactured in Germany up to the end of the First World War, one third were either intact or had been dismantled. Throughout the war, not one Zeppelin had been lost due to any sort of engineering failure. On the other hand, an alarming one-in-three airships had been lost due to operating errors (from heavy landings to hangar fires), which was marginally more than the number lost by enemy action!

«L14-L41-L42-L52-L56 L63-L65»

The final casualties. The frail structure of airships was demonstrated on 23 June 1919, after the German surrender. The airship bases were under the control of 'Sailors' Soviets' but the flying crews – especially the regulars – were determined to prevent their airships being turned over to the victors.

The crews went to the hangars, and for the last time hoisted the war ensign of the Imperial German Navy on each airship. The supports were pulled clear and the suspension tackles loosened from the roofs of the cathedral-like sheds. The crews were silent as the Zeppelins crashed to the hangar

Top: A Royal Navy Camel biplane lands on HMS *Furious*.

Centre: L63 and L65 *(bottom)* wrecked in their sheds. The gas cells were not inflated, so severing their supports caused their total destruction.

floors. The fall, of less than 6 feet, was enough to reduce the 40-ton weight of finely balanced structure into a total wreck.

The L61 at Wittmundhaven escaped destruction because she was flown by von Schiller for a film!

The bombing airship was obsolete by then. The technology of airships had developed during the war but the aeroplane had progressed even faster. Of the big, 2-million-cubic-foot Zeppelins that were flying from May 1916 onwards, one out of every five was shot down by an aeroplane.

The British navy's ambition to own rigid airships had to some extent evaporated during the very long time the factories took to build them. Britain's first wartime rigid flew in November 1916 and was a copy of the long-obsolete Zeppelin ZIV, which had been examined after a forced landing in Luneville, France, in April 1913. The few British rigids that followed were similarly impractical. They were too heavy, leaving no margin for payload. None of them was suitable for war service.

These Sea Scout airships had no rigid structure. Even a slight loss of gas caused them to buckle.

– some no more than a crude envelope supporting an obsolete wingless aeroplane. But they were effective, and the men who manned these curious contraptions had their own airship stories to tell.

One of the tiny Sea Scout class airships was landing at Llangefni, near Anglesey, late in 1916. She had been on a routine anti-submarine patrol over the Irish Sea. During the landing, the three-man airship hit and killed a cow. The wireless operator jumped out. Thus lightened, the airship went up rapidly.

The engine had stopped and she was out of control. She was blown out to sea until she flew low enough to touch the waves. Then the engineer was thrown into the sea by the impact. Again the airship was lightened, and flew away with only the pilot aboard. Eventually she hit the sea again. This time she broke up but the third member of the crew, F/Sub. Lt. A. D. A. M. Young, clung to the wreckage until a passing ship rescued him. The engineer was never found.

«SEA SCOUTS» More important to
Britain's war effort were 200 cheap little blimps, used for anti-submarine patrols and convoy protection

«R34» A perfect landing. R34 was the
first airship to cross the Atlantic. Like her sister ship, R33, she was a wartime copy of the Zeppelin L33 shot down in September 1916.

Left: R34 was the first airship to cross the Atlantic. Its end came when wind beat the nose of the moored airship against the ground.

The end of the R34 came in January 1921, about eighteen months after the Atlantic flight. Loaned to the RAF, she left Howden base in Yorkshire at noon on 27 January with student navigators aboard, and flew east over the North Sea.

The wireless gave trouble and it was late that night before the airship returned across the Yorkshire coastline to reports of worsening weather. Her cruising altitude over the sea had been 1,200 feet and she did not climb, although the Yorkshire Moors rise in places to 1,400 feet.

About midnight the airship hit a hillside. The control car 'scooped up heather' and propeller blades shattered. Deprived of forward speed, the airship drifted upwards and was blown out to sea by a stiff breeze.

The crew checked the airship and found that, although three engines were out of action, there was very little other damage. In spite of the bad weather, they made slow progress back home using the two remaining engines. At Howden the R34 made a perfect landing with the aid of an experienced mooring party of about 400 men. But the wind gusting off the hangar walls made it impossible to walk the airship back into her shed.

There was no alternative but to moor the airship in the open. As wind gusts reached 30 m.p.h. the nose of the airship was beaten against the ground. One of the forward gas bags was punctured and the rudder jammed hard over to port causing the airship to swing against her mooring lines. Soon the airship's mooring point was torn loose and the nose collapsed completely. The airship was then destroyed by men who were sent in to rip the fabric back and chop the alloy framework with axes.

«R33»

A happy ending. These copies of the sophisticated German R class had been modified for five engines instead of six,

with a corresponding loss of speed. But the 2-million-cubic-feet capacity was the same. However, the ships had standing orders that no one aboard one of them must ever run, and never must more than four men go aft of frame 33, for fear that the weight change might unbalance the ship.

But the finely balanced structures could take considerable punishment along normal lines of stress, as the R33 had proved on 16 April 1925 by riding out two days of fierce storm at her mast.

The crew, but not the captain, were aboard at 9.50 that morning as violent gusts from different directions tore the nose off the mast. The first officer

Left: The British airship R33 had its nose moored to a mast when violent gusts of wind lifted it up into the sky. In spite of considerable damage to its frame and gas cells, it got back to earth safely *(right)*.

took command. He said, 'The top of the mast was carried away first. The ship, then being slightly heavy at the nose, crashed down to the railings which surround the top of the mast, and these broke the bow.'

The jagged end of the girder bent inwards to puncture the front gas bag and it was leaking badly as the airship lifted away, nose heavy. From the control car the commander released the forward water ballast. This quick action saved the ship, for as she passed over the hangars and wind-screens there was little space to spare. In the engine cars the mechanics were working furiously; one engine was running within two minutes of the breakaway, and all were turning one minute later.

The 30-year-old first officer, commanding a rigid for the first time, inspected the nose from the inside. It was badly damaged.

When he went out on top, and walked as far as he dared towards it, he could not see the full extent of the crushed nose. But he knew the loss of gas from number one cell was severe and he would have to do something to prevent a gust of wind coming in through the torn cover and ripping the rest of the gas cells open. He ordered that the punctured gas cell – now empty – should be laced to the number two frame, to make a false nose. The cover was draped over the damaged girders.

The wind did not lessen. The first officer kept the engines turning slowly (a proven good measure in almost any airship emergency) and the wind pushed the airship out over the North Sea. Going backwards sometimes, the R33 was blown all the way to Holland before the weather improved enough for the engines to get a grip on the wind.

On the afternoon of the next day, having spent nearly thirty hours in the air, the R33 was safely landed again. The crew received a message of appreciation from the King, and a watch.

R33 survived from 1919 to 1928, and its 800 hours, although negligible in comparison with the *Graf Zeppelin*'s record, was the longest flying time of any British rigid. When R33 died, she died of old age. Gas bags did not last much more than three years and most structures weakened after five.

«R38» Like a cracked egg.

As the war ended, the British government used its emergency powers to take over Shorts. Out of this unhappy situation came the R38, an airship for which were claimed all kinds of radical new ideas but which was in effect a copy of the Zeppelin technology. Had it been only that, many lives would have been saved but the men who designed the R38 were ordered to produce an airship that could take a work-load to 22,000 feet. The result was the largest airship so far built.

The USA had no rigid airships and an attempt to have one built by the Zeppelin company was countermanded by the authorities because the USA and Germany were technically still at war.

As the British began to close down their airship programme the Americans offered to buy the still unfinished R38. By the summer of 1921 an American crew had been trained, and although the ship was not yet handed over to the USA, the R38 was painted in USA markings.

There were 17 Americans aboard her on the final test-flight, together with 28 British crew, the designer, and some laboratory workers equipped to measure the stresses during turns and speed tests.

On 23 August 1921 the R38 flew out over the North Sea and spent a day and night in the air. The following morning the speed trials recorded a commendable 71 m.p.h. and a radio message from her reported that the trials were complete. All that remained was for the ship to be officially handed over so that the American sailors could fly her home.

Right: R38 snapped in two before falling into the water near Hull, Yorkshire

The weather was perfect that afternoon as the biggest flying machine the world had yet seen cruised low over the city of Hull, Yorkshire. Who gave the order to execute a series of violent turns has never been discovered. Certainly no survivor took responsibility.

They were at 2,500 feet as the rudder man turned his control wheel all the way to port, and then all the way to starboard, and back again. The airship shuddered. No airship could take that sort of treatment. Even the steel hull of a destroyer would buckle if used in that way.

The men in the control car heard a sound like gunfire; the girders were buckling and snapping apart. The nose dropped suddenly and the captain ordered ballast to be discharged to right her, not realising that his airship was breaking in two. She parted in the middle, 'like a cracked egg,' said one witness, who saw it from the ground. And out of the broken shell came furniture, bedding, broken fragments and men. A parachute opened. Another, shared by two men, fell swiftly to the fast tidal water of the estuary.

As the two halves of the airship separated, there were still the sinewy threads of bracing wires, fuel lines and electric cables stretching between. As these snapped, sharp edges tore into the fragile gas cells and released hydrogen into the air.

Side-by-side along the keel, ruptured fuel lines spewed their contents upon the torn electric cables. The flames ignited the hydrogen, and the front section of the airship caught fire as it tumbled out of the sky. There was an explosion, violent enough to break shop windows in the city, and then another as the nose part hit the water and splashed flaming fuel over the few swimming survivors.

The after section did not catch fire. The buoyancy of its few intact gas cells made it fall more slowly, and on a level keel. Men inside it came rushing forward towards the control car, where some parachutes were stowed. They were amazed to find blinding daylight and empty space. 'There's nothing there,' shouted one of them.

The tail of the airship touched down gently. Some survivors jumped, and found themselves on a spit of sand, the water no more than three or four feet deep. Others, inside the tangled mess of wires, fabric and twisted girders, were not so lucky. They were still inside when the wind rolled the wreckage along to deeper water, where it sank.

From the front section only one man survived: the captain. From the rear there were four survivors. Of the seventeen Americans only one got out alive.

After the crash it was revealed by the Aeronautical Research Committee that aerodynamic forces had been omitted from the design calculations. The R38 was never actually handed over to the Americans but they got the bill for it; the airship cost them $884,095.62, and there were another $98,069.06 for training.

«ZR1.SHENANDOAH»

Going to the Fair. The R38 had crashed by the time *Shenandoah* – 'Daughter of the Stars' – was ready to fly. This airship was the first rigid built in the USA. Parts made in the Philadelphia navy aircraft factory were assembled in a big hangar at Lakehurst, New Jersey.

Shenandoah was based upon the design of the German navy's L49 which had been force-landed in France in October 1917. But the height climber had been considerably modified: she needed an extra section because the Americans filled her with non-inflammable helium which had less lift. *Shenandoah* was the first airship to use it.

She was the finest publicity device the US navy

Shenandoah at her mobile mooring mast at sea.

OHIO'S
GREATEST HOME
DAILY

Columbus Evening Dispatch.

FULL PAGE OF PICTURES
Interesting photographs of events and persons are contained in a full page feature in The Dispatch daily.

WEATHER—Fair tonight. Friday fair and cooler.　　　COLUMBUS, OHIO, THURSDAY, SEPTEMBER 3, 1925.　　　VOL. LV. NO. 65.　**　PRICE TWO CENTS.

SHENANDOAH, TWISTED BY SQUALL, PLUNGES DOWN IN THREE PIECES

FOURTEEN MEMBERS OF CREW INCLUDING LT. COM. LANSDOWNE KILLED NEAR CALDWELL, OHIO

Most of Dead are Found in Wreckage of Control Cabin Which Dropped in Cornfield on Outskirts of Ava

TAIL SECTION DRIFTS 12 MILES

Out of Control in High Wind, Big Dirigible Bumps Ground Several Times and Then Seals Fate by Crashing into Walnut Tree

THE DEAD.

Lieutenant Commander Zachary Lansdowne, Greenville, Ohio, commanding officer.

Lieutenant Commander Louis Hancock, Austin, Tex., second in command.

Lieut. J. B. Lawrence, St. Paul, Minn., senior watch officer.

Lieut. A. R. Houghton, Allston, Mass., watch officer.

Everette P. Allen, Omaha, Neb., aviation chief rigger.

Charles Broom, Toms River, N. J., aviation chief machinist mate.

James W. Cullinan, Binghamton, N. Y., aviation pilot.

Ralph T. Joffray, St. Louis, Mo., aviation rigger.

Celestino P. Mazzuco, Murray Hill, N. J., aviation machinist mate.

James A. Moore, Jr., Savannah, Ga., aviation machinist mate.

Bartholomew O'Sullivan, Lowell. Mass., aviation machinist mate.

George C. Schnitzer, Tuckerton. N. J., chief radio man.

William H. Spratley, St. Louis, Mo., aviation machinist mate, first class.

Lieut. E. W. Sheppard, Washington, D. C., engineer officer.

THE INJURED.

Raymond Cole, Lima, Ohio, radio officer.

John F. McCarthy, Boston, Mass., aviation chief rigger.

CALDWELL, OHIO, SEPT. 3.—(AP)—The giant dirigible Shenandoah is no more. It went down in three pieces here early today and killed its commander, Lieutenant Commander Zachary Lansdowne and at least 13 of the officers and men, making up her crew.

The airship struck a line squall—a variety of storm much feared by airmen—shortly after 5 o'clock this morning in the Noble county village, while traveling

SHENANDOAH AS IT APPEARED BEFORE CRASH

COMMANDER ZACHARY LANSDOWNE

Aboard the navy dirigible Shenandoah when it was wrecked near Cambridge, Ohio, Thursday morning maintained a residence at 338 East Third street, Greenville, Ohio. Other Ohioans in the crew were Ray-

EYE-WITNESS TELLS HOW HE SAW AIR MONSTER FALTER, BREAK, AND SLIP TO EARTH

C. L. Arthur Declares Tragedy Was Preceded by Muffled Roar; Gondola Carrying 13 Dashed to Ground Like Egg-Shell

BELLE VALLEY, OHIO, SEPT. 3.—A great cigar-shaped monster, its sides shimmering like silver in the first rays of the dawn, as it glided gracefully through the heavens. A muffled roar which echoed and re-echoed through the silent country side. A drunken careening hulk aloft where the dirigible seemed to momentarily stand still and then—not a crash—but a seemingly gentle slipping to earth.

This was the picture of the wreck of the Shenandoah, pride of the United States navy, painted here today by C. L. Arthur of this town.

PASSENGER HURTLED OUT.

"Then the rest of the ship continued in a southerly direction, blown rapidly by the terrific wind. It skirted the tops of the trees in a heavy wood and sank lower as it passed over a plowed field adjoining. As it passed over the trees, somehow—just why we did not find out—one of the passengers came hurt-

"It was impossible to get the men out of the gondola without getting the thing down so we got guns and shot the gas bag full of holes. It then fell to the ground and we were able to extricate the six passengers from the wreckage. All of these were in rather precarious condition.

SHENANDOAH TRAGEDY STORY IS ONE OF HEROISM OF CREW WHO FOUGHT STORM IN VAIN

Col. C. G. Hall Tells of Thrilling Battle Put Up by Men Who Dangle on Ropes and Ladders High in the Air

AIR CURRENTS TOO STRONG

Blames Failure of Meteorological Stations to Warn Dirigible of Dangerous Conditions of Atmosphere

CALDWELL, OHIO, SEPT. 3.—The story of the Shenandoah disaster, in which the giant dirigible crashed and broke into three portions over Ava, Ohio, near here, this morning, resulting in the death of 14 aboard the airship, is one of heroism of the crew, pioneers in the interest of the development of lighter-than-air transportation. It is best told by Col. C. G. Hall, U. S. army observer aboard the ill-fated ship.

"We were traveling west at an altitude of about 3000 feet when we encountered a storm," Col Hall said in describing the accident. "By changing our course a dozen or more times, we dodged it, only to encounter

Navy Department Hears That Lightning Wrecked Big Dirigible

WASHINGTON, SEPT. 3.—(AP)—The Moundsville, W. Va., aviation field telegraphed the navy department today that the Shenandoah was "struck by lightning" at 5:35 o'clock this morning.

The message indicated the information had been obtained from army aviators who had gone to the scene.

"Shenandoah struck by lightning," the message said, "during storm at 5:35 a. m. today near Pleasant City, Ohio, south of Cambridge. Ship cut in half. One part down at Pleasant City. Other part down at Berne, about two miles east of Caldwell, Ohio. Positions verified by Major Kerr, air service, flying from Fairfield to Langin this a. m."

had ever known. Even the admirals who despised airships saw the value of one with US Navy painted on the side, floating above the heads of voters who lived a thousand miles from the coast.

Shenandoah's fatal flight took her over a region notorious for violent storms, and at a time when a cyclonic storm area was moving towards them. Her captain was doubtful but the navy's top brass were delighted with the prospect of showing the airship to five State Fairs and forty cities, and all in six days.

Storms were nothing new to the farmers of Ohio, especially in September, but one or two observers in Noble County that night in 1925 noted a strange phenomenon; black storm clouds were racing from both north and south, to meet above their heads.

The crew of the airship were undaunted by the lightning that flickered along the horizon. They were more concerned with the headwind that held them almost stationary over the moonlit landscape. The airship was exactly two years old that day, and she had flown 25,000 miles in all kinds of weather, including storms.

It was daybreak as the first sign of trouble came to men in the control car. The elevator man told the captain that the ship was rising in spite of everything he did. He kept turning the wheel, so that finally the airship was nose-down by 18 degrees, yet still she was going up. The dials showed she was moving up at 2 metres per second. The captain swung the telegraph to bring the engines up to full speed.

Shenandoah continued to rise. She had entered a freak confluence of air. A river of cold air coming south was overriding another warmer air stream coming north. As the warm air went up, *Shenandoah* was going with it. From the ground some farmers already awake watched the airship, and saw a dark line-squall forming over the top of her.

In spite of the steep angle of the airship and her violent movement, the crew went about their duties without alarm. On number two engine, the chief noticed that the radiator was about to boil over. He closed the throttle and climbed the steep ladder back into the airship to get water.

In the control car the engineering officer phoned from Frame 105 (105 metres from the tail) and gave the order to 'dope the fuel tanks'. Putting ethyl lead into the fuel was an emergency measure and a sign that the airship was in trouble.

But the most vital task at that moment was given to the men on their way to rip the 'jam pot covers' off the emergency gas valves. The cost of the helium had persuaded the airship commanders to reduce the number of automatic release valves in the airship, and put jam pot covers over others. At first the seals had only been on while the airship was grounded but recently they stayed on during flight. Now the airship was rising rapidly. If she went past 'pressure height' where the thinner air allowed the helium to distend and totally fill the sealed bags, the airship would expand and tear herself to pieces.

She was at 3,000 feet when the altimeter steadied. The airship was rolling and pitching worse than ever before. If the men watching the altimeter breathed a sigh of relief it was only a short breath for soon the airship lurched and continued upwards. The men in the control car opened all the manoeuvring valves, and held them open. The precious helium was venting but the airship was rising more quickly than ever, at 1,000 feet per minute. The airship passed pressure height and was at 6,000 feet before she fell back towards the dawn-streaked farmland of Ohio. She was heavy now – 7,370 lbs heavy – and she dropped with a speed that made the eardrums pop and the belly weaken. Only the

48

Right: Shenandoah.

discharge of 4,370 lbs of ballast checked the fall.

But *Shenandoah* was now the plaything of a vast mass of turbulent air. The physics of lifting gas, the aerodynamics of the profile and the weight of water were all meaningless rituals being played out by a doomed crew. At 3,000 feet she was tossed back into the upper air again, and gusts of wind started to spin the giant ship, as a ball-player might apply break to a ball. She was nearly 700 feet long but went spinning through the storm clouds with the nose pointing up at thirty degrees. And then with the terrible sounds of fracturing girders and 'a combination of noises hard to describe' this giant airship was torn into two pieces.

She broke at Frame 125 – about a third of the way from the front – but for a moment the two parts were held together by the steel control wires that joined the huge rudders and elevators of the tail to the control car suspended under the airship's nose. Falling asunder, the cables snatched the control car off its supports with such force that the men inside it were catapulted into space.

The engineering officer was standing at the place where the break happened. He embraced the girders of the bow section as it broke away. The girders round him crumpled too. Men forward of him tried to grab him but he told them, 'Never mind me, look out for yourself.' They said he was still gripping pieces of wire and metal in his dead hands when they found him.

After the engineering officer fell, there were seven men in the huge bow section of the airship. Its gas cells were intact and without the weight of the control car it ascended rapidly. No one knows how high it went – some say to 10,000 feet.

The rear of the broken airship – about two-thirds of her length – fractured again as the two forward engine cars, and their 300 h.p. Packards and 10-foot-long propellers, fell off, taking the mechanics with them. The ruptured tail section had gas cells still intact. It did not fall. It separated into two, and both drifted down to the ground. The wind dragged them across hills and woodland leaving behind a trail of dead and injured men.

As the sky lightened, men on the ground looked up through the grey drizzle of rain and watched the amazing sight of the bow section – 225 feet long – spinning like a top through the sky as if it would never return to earth. In it, the seven men, sick, shaken and dizzy from the whirling motion, clung tightly to the broken wires and girders and took orders from the senior officer.

It was two hours from the time that the control car hit the ground that the bow section touched down 12 miles away. All that time the shattered piece of airship danced and tumbled round Ohio in great 10-mile circles.

Crouched inside the framework, wedged between the bent girders and billowing gas bags, the sailors hung on tightly, and secured their comrades. As ordered, they valved off the helium, stilled the spinning and brought the last segment of 'Daughter of the Stars' to earth. But after two hours of terror one of the survivors grabbed a farmer's shotgun and blasted the remaining gas cells, so that no part of her would ever leave earth again.

Left: The wreckage of the American airship *Shenandoah* in Ohio.

50

«N2. ITALIA»

The fatal sunlight. The last flight of the airship *Italia* is the stuff of which nightmares are made. General Nobile, an Italian airship designer, was commanding an expedition to the North Pole. The airship was a small semi-rigid – a blimp with a keel – and aboard were sixteen men, fourteen of them Italian.

On 23 May 1928 the airship left Spitsbergen and reached the Pole as planned, considerably assisted by a brisk, following wind. The airship did not land at the Pole but she hovered while ceremonies and scientific experiments were conducted. It was a good chance to test the extent and force of the earth's magnetic field.

When it was time to move on, Nobile decided to return to Spitsbergen rather than press on towards North America. The decision was made in the light of the Swedish meteorologists' assurance that the wind would not last. But the wind did last, and now *Italia* was flying into it. The ground speed was almost zero.

In a combination of weather conditions that perhaps only the Arctic regions experience, the gale-force winds were accompanied by dense fog. The need to check the speed and drift of the airship (done by marking the ground and taking sights on the mark) forced them to descend through the fog. The glare of the light inside the cloud made it difficult to see the limitless pack-ice below them. They were dangerously low, at about 500 feet, as they levelled off to take the sightings.

Even without the sightings it was obvious to everyone aboard that their progress was no more than a snail's pace. It was as if the airship was pressing against an invisible wall of wind. None of Nobile's attempts to steer round the wind succeeded. Worse, there was the continuous build-up of ice, not only on the wires and girders but also on the envelope itself. The outer covering of the airship had been specially strengthened but fragments of ice thrown off the propellers were going right through it and puncturing the gas cells. Each time this happened the leaks had to be found and mended immediately.

The ice eventually jammed the elevators and *Italia* descended towards the ice pack. Disobeying orders, one of the crew threw cans of fuel overboard. He was reprimanded but it was enough to lighten the airship and this time she rose up so high that she broke out of the top of the clouds into blinding sunshine. The proximity of magnetic north made any compass reading unreliable but now, while the elevators were being repaired, there was a chance to get a 'line of position' by taking a reading from the sun.

When the airship went down into the chilly clouds again, she was heavy, and even putting the engines to full speed did not help very much. With nose up-tilted, and engines roaring, the *Italia* continued to sink until she came out through the bottom of the cloud base.

The airship hit the ice with a tremendous crash, ripping away the rear engine car and killing the mechanic. Dragging across the ice ridges the control car, too, was torn away from the keel. One wall

General Nobile. He took an unfair share of the blame for the *Italia* disaster.

Left: The *Italia* at Spitsbergen before departure for the North Pole.

of the car was still hanging from the airship as she rose up into the sky, lightened by having lost the weight of men and equipment that were scattered across the ice.

Looking down at the scene from the airship there were six of the crew. The airship was now no more than a free balloon, and the wind snatched her up and carried her off towards the North Pole. *Italia* – and the six men – disappeared into the fog, and no trace was ever seen again.

Afterwards the experts argued about the cause of the crash. Hugo Eckener said that the airship must have gone through 'pressure height'. The sun warming the hydrogen caused it to continue to expand and so continue to vent through the automatic valves. By the time the airship descended into the colder air she had so little lift that she could not even carry her own weight. From that moment a crash was inevitable.

Nobile and the nine survivors remained on the ice for nearly a month. One died. There was a loss of life in the search party, too. After the men were found there were bitter recriminations, and some critics suggested that the six men who had floated away might really have been eaten by the survivors. Nobile, seen here recuperating from his ordeal, became a convenient scapegoat for the whole disaster.

«R101» Lord Thomson's route to India.

In 1924 the British government decided to build two modern rigid airships as the beginning of an air-line between London and India and eventually between London and Australia. Unfortunately this Labour government decided that the airship programme could provide a competition between the 'socialist' R101 to be built at the nationalised airship works, and the 'capitalist' R100 built by a private company.

The way in which the R38 and the *Shenandoah* had broken up in mid-air haunted the designers. These new airships gained extra strength from their swelling profiles (each ring was a different size) and the R101 was built with stainless-steel girders as well as with lightweight duralumin.

Each and every one of the new ideas to be embodied in the 'socialist' airship was given great publicity through official outlets. One of these ideas was that diesel engines used non-inflammable' diesel oil, so were the only sort suitable for tropical flights. The only type of diesels anywhere near suitable for the airship were originally intended for locomotives. They weighed 17 tons and provided disappointing power. But the Air Ministry bureaucrats were adamant about letting the R101 change to petrol engines. All concerned had been trapped by their own publicity.

The most fundamental design departure was in the rings of the airship. Not only were they all different sizes (which meant separate calculations and separate construction) but they were without bracing wires.

These wires – like the spokes of a bicycle wheel – not only permitted the German designers to keep the outer rings light but also kept the gas cells apart. The R101's drum-shaped gas bags each needed a 'hairnet' anchoring them to the framework, lest they surge backwards and forwards

through the rings. And the stronger rings used up space that would otherwise be used for gas, depriving the airship of about 15 tons of lift. For the gas cells a new sort of valve had been invented. It was so sensitive that very small pressure variations, or an inclination of only three degrees, would cause it to release gas.

By October 1929 the R101 was able to fly – but only just. The weight of the stainless steel, the larger rings, the reduced gas capacity, the weight of the diesel engines and many new devices such as the power steering system, all militated on the side of gravity. Not only did the airship prove to be 23 tons heavier than the calculations predicted but there were 1½ tons less lift too.

There was no suggestion of scrapping this white elephant. The Labour government had staked too much on its success and half-a-million pounds of public money had already been spent on her. Instead they lightened ship; throwing out the expensive power steering and all the other disposable weight. Then they loosened the 'hairnets' so that they could get more gas into the bags, and finally they sliced her in half and inserted a whole new bay.

All the time the Labour Air Minister, who had now become Lord Thomson of Cardington (having adopted the name of the nationalised airship factory as his title), was pressing for an early departure to India. He must be back in London by mid-October for the Imperial Conference. Less charitable voices said that he was determined to be the next Viceroy of India. A triumphant flight to India and back, in the airship that was his personal project, might be a part of that ambitious plan.

Lord Thomson's sense of urgency was not reduced by the way the 'capitalist' sister ship, having cost the taxpayer rather less than the R101, took off in July 1930 and flew to Canada and back.

The R101's outer cover, a vital protection for the

Lord Thomson, Secretary of State for Air, lost his life when disaster overtook the R101 on her maiden flight to India.

Left: When the inferno subsided, R101 lay sprawled across a hillside in Northern France like the bleached bones of a stranded whale.

fragile gas bags inside, had been a source of constant trouble. As the airship came out of her hangar in June 1930, a rip nearly 50 yards long appeared. Next day it tore again. Repairs using rubber solution caused a chemical reaction with the dope. The fabric rotted and much of it was replaced. There were also stories of construction workers urinating on the cover rather than climb all the way down to the hangar floor to use the toilets.

On 1 October 1930 the newly lightened, newly lengthened, newly covered R101 made a trial flight. An oil-cooler broke down and without that engine she couldn't do the speed trials. But Lord Thomson was by now insistent that the flight must start within a day or two. The pressures from above became so great that a Certificate of Airworthiness was issued without an inspector's report. There was a verbal provision that the speed test must be done during the flight to India, and the airship should turn back if it wasn't satisfactory. When one considers how the French might have felt about an airship with a bogus Certificate of Airworthiness, but with a full complement of passengers, doing test flights over their heads, it is understandable that this provision was not included in the written instructions given to the airship commander.

On the evening of 4 October 1930 the R101 lifted very slowly away from her mast at the Royal Airship Works, Cardington. She was the largest airship in the world; about double the gas capacity of the *Graf Zeppelin* and 777 feet long. Aboard, on their way to India, were the designer, official guests, Lord Thomson and his valet and a crew of 42 men.

The night was dark and stormy and the airship had to discharge nearly half-a-ton of water ballast before she was light enough to lift away. She went slowly and disappeared into the racing grey clouds. This airship had never known this kind of weather, and soon after take-off a revised weather forecast predicted winds of 40–50 m.p.h. over France. The airship was rolling and pitching worse than ever before and the loosened 'hairnets' allowed the gas bags to surge. This caused the airship to snake through the air in continuous climbs and dives. And every time she tilted more than three degrees, the sensitive valves released hydrogen the airship could not spare.

Over London the rain beat down upon the cover, adding the weight of tons of water. Soon one of the engines gave trouble and had to be stopped for repairs. As the airship crossed the Channel the men working on the engine glanced down and saw the rough water surprisingly close under them. In the control car, an officer grabbed the elevator wheel from the helmsman and brought the airship up to 1,000 feet.

As they crossed France, the winds increased. Heavy with rain, the airship lost height. At Poix airfield they said she was not more than 300 feet above the ground. The surging gas bags, and the general instability of the ship caused her to wallow so much that some observers on the ground thought her lights were going on and off.

At two o'clock in the morning, the watch changed. Five minutes after this the airship went into a dive that was more alarming than her previous flight path. The officer on watch ordered full up-elevator and brought the engines to half speed. From the control car there was no way of releasing the last of the forward water ballast (some ballast had already been used to lift off the mast). A rigger went forward to do it by hand. Some of the crew were awakened by the coxswain running through the airship shouting, 'We're down, lads'; and then came the impact.

Slightly nose-down, the R101 hit a hillside near Beauvais, France. Thanks to the elevator man, who died holding the wheel to climb position, the huge

Right: After lying in state in Beauvais Town Hall, the 44 coffins bearing the remains of the dead from R101 were conveyed with full military honours on horse-drawn artillery wagons to a special train bound for Boulogne.

airship touched the ground lightly and at no more than walking pace. From the port amidships engine gondola, a man jumped out and ran. The airship, sucked along perhaps by the wind blowing over the ridge, touched the ground and bounced about 60 feet into the air. As she came down again her back broke at the place where the new bay had been inserted.

For a moment there was only the noise of falling rain, then came the roar of 5 million cubic feet of flaming hydrogen. Two men trapped by the flames in an aft engine gondola alongside 30 gallons of petrol (for the starting motor) were saved by the sudden drenching that a water-ballast bag gave them.

More desperate still was the plight of a man trapped inside the asbestos-walled smoking room, deep inside the gas envelope. He heard the thunder of flaming gas, but the distortion of the ship's frame had jammed the door tightly shut. Desperately he kicked his way through the asbestos walls. Under him there were flames. He jumped into them, went through the burning structure and landed in wet trees.

Of the 54 persons aboard, only 6 survived. Few of the dead were recognisable. Next day the mess of metal was still hot and the hillside flickered with mysterious patches of flame; it was diesel fuel from the heavy engines.

At Karachi the great airship hangar awaited the arrival of the R101. It is still there today, empty and unused. At the public inquiry a new fact emerged, although it must have been known to all the senior men at the Air Ministry. Calculations (based upon forty years of weather reports) proved that the R101 could never have operated a regular service through Karachi. The hot weather over most of the year would have deprived the airship of so much lift that she could never have carried the necessary fuel.

«R100» Executed on official orders.

For nearly three decades airships had been shaped like tubes with equal-sized rings. This had enabled the Germans to build their airships in just a few weeks by 'mass producing' identical rings. Also these tube-shaped airships gave the maximum possible gas capacity for the dimensions of the shed.

But most airship experts (Eckener was a notable exception) agreed that a swelling profile would be more efficient, providing less air-resistance and some aerodynamic lift, of the sort an aeroplane gets from its shaped wings. The first design of this new sort was the R80 that an Englishman Dr Barnes Wallis submitted in 1916. But this excellent airship didn't fly until 1920. By this time the Zeppelin Company had their streamlined *Bodensee* flying. It proved the value of the new profile by establishing an airship speed record of 82.4 m.p.h.

When Barnes Wallis was employed to build the 'capitalist' R100, he made it the plumpest airship ever built. And he considered it a personal responsibility. 'I designed every part in that ship myself,' he later said. (Richmond, on the other airship, was not a designer and worked as the manager of a team of experts. So, as Wallis's biographer says, it was not only a competition between capitalism and socialism, but between team-work and an individual brilliance.)

The R100 was a mixture of audacious inventions and money-saving austerity. There were only 11 different parts, and 15 different joints, in the entire structure. Standard metal-thickness made calculations exact and simple. Barnes Wallis devised a helical tube, made from riveted strip, to fashion girders of his own design. On the other hand, having brushed aside the Air Ministry's observations about petrol engines in the tropics, he used second-hand reconditioned petrol engines for his

Barnes Wallis, young apprentice on the *Mayfly*, designed the R100.

airship. A great admirer of Count Zeppelin, Barnes Wallis was not too proud to have parts of his airship made in Germany.

The resulting airship was good enough to cross the Atlantic in the summer of 1930, although by then three other airships had done the same. On her return she was put into her shed and never flew again. Angry, sad and disappointed about the tragedy of the R101, the politicians ordered that R100 should be broken up and sold for scrap. A steam roller was used to crush the frail alloy pieces.

The whole episode of the R100 created a bitter memory for many, as evidenced by this poem that appeared at the time.

She was alive – and they hated her,
    Willed her as dead as their wits!
They knew how highly men rated her –
    So now she is lying in bits.
For she was the work of their masters,
    Whose mastery put them to shame,
She gave them no dower of disasters
    So they made her one – hacksaw and flame!

Four hundred thousands of money,
    Two generations of brain,
And the ways and the means and the money
    Have all to be called for again!
Airworthy, tried and found trusty,
    She showed up a ship that was not,
They knew she would never rot rusty –
    So a steamroller rolls o'er the lot!

«ZR4.AKRON» Thunderstorms

from Washington. For the USA, the rigid airship had brought tragedy. The R38 had broken up over Britain, *Shenandoah* had been destroyed in a storm in Ohio. Only the German-made Zeppelin, *Los Angeles*, remained in the American skies.

In 1926 the US government agreed to build two new airships for the US Navy. They would be designed for the non-inflammable helium gas that only the USA had, and this enabled the eight engines to be inside the hull. In the *Shenandoah* disaster, all but three deaths had been due to the cars being severed from their suspensions; the new airships would have crew accommodation inside the hull, and the control car fixed directly to the nose.

A radical departure was the aircraft hangar inside the airship. It could hold four or five small biplane fighters which flew on and off the airship at will. Using these, the airship could search a lane 100 miles wide, at a speed of about 75 m.p.h.

There were resemblances to the R100 and R101. There was steel in the structure and the rings were unwired. The profile was like the British airships too; *Akron* was 5.9 times as long as it was wide, and a dramatic change from *Shenandoah*'s 'fineness ratio' of 1 to 8.7.

The propellers could swivel to provide thrust upwards, downwards, forwards and back. So much care was taken about the outer cover that the men fitting it practised for three weeks before working on the airship. *Akron* was as good as technology permitted. Filled with the non-inflammable helium gas there was every reason to claim that the airship had been perfected.

In April 1933, when the airship was about eighteen months old, it left Lakehurst (about 50 miles south of New York City) on a flight to calibrate the radio-direction-finding stations along the New England coast.

The weather report showed a cold front of considerable length, approaching from the west. Thunderstorms from Washington were moving north-east towards them. The air was thick with static, so there would be no chance of calibrating

Two young seamen lost their lives when they fell 200 feet from the *Akron*'s mooring lines as the airship suddenly rose into the air while attempting a landing near San Diego, California.

the radio-direction-finding stations for a couple of days. There was also fog over Lakehurst, from 300 feet to 1,500.

Admiral Moffett, Chief of the Bureau of Aeronautics and an advocate of airships, had arranged to join the airship for this flight, so in spite of the difficulties it was decided to leave as scheduled. To avoid the storms they would fly inland, south of the moving thunderstorms, and then come north, so that the New England coast would be the final segment of a gigantic circle, reached long after the disturbances had disappeared out into the Atlantic Ocean.

At 7.28 p.m. on 2 April 1933 Akron lifted away from the US navy's airship base at Lakehurst, New Jersey. They headed inland, as planned, and saw the great city of Philadelphia under them. There, they turned south-west to follow the wide River Delaware. Near Wilmington the men in the control car saw lightning flashes to the south. They realised that the cold front, causing the storms, was far more extensive than they had calculated. The executive officer suggested that they turn due west again but before they could do this, the western sky was also marked with the scratches of distant lightning.

Even as they watched, the storms extended, until the whole horizon of the south and the west was marked by lightning. There was no alternative but to fly away from it as fast and as directly as possible. Akron headed north-east, back the way it had come, climbing to 1,600 feet to get over the thick layer of fog that marked the Atlantic coast. By 10 p.m. they had crossed the coast and were heading due east. The captain told his executive officer that they would fly well out over the Atlantic. Since the storm was heading north-east, they would get out of its way, and let it pass behind them.

However, the men in the control car could not be certain what the storms were doing; the electrical interference spoiled much of the 10 p.m. weather report, although they did hear that a low-pressure area was centred on Washington. And that same static prevented them from getting a fix on the radio-direction-finding stations too. They could no longer be certain of their own position.

By 11 p.m. lightning had been seen on all sides of the airship. The confused weather pattern persuaded the captain to head back towards the land until he could see the coastline. They picked up the lights of the coast but rather than risk a collision with the New York skyscrapers (actually the airship was a long way farther south than the navigator thought) they turned out to sea again. This time heading south-east in another attempt to get behind the storms.

They were attempting the impossible. The cold front was far too long to escape. By now Akron was flying through heavy rain, and the barometer needle swung crazily as the storms approached. There is nowhere else in the world that has cold fronts, and the associated phenomena, like this part of the USA. The cold air mass was spilling out over the Atlantic, prising up the unsettled warm air into storm clouds and turbulence. On the airship, men began to feel the uncertain support that the mixed air provided, as the decks pitched and rolled underfoot. As a safety measure, the wireless aerials were drawn in. Now the airship could neither send nor receive messages.

At fifteen minutes past midnight, some 30 miles out over the Atlantic, Akron hit an air-pocket that dropped her through the sky. Ballast was discharged immediately, and the airship slowed her descent and recovered. In the control car they watched the altimeter needle go down as far as 700 feet above sea level, then steady itself.

Almost immediately the airship was nosing into

Right: The awesome size of the airships is shown by this photograph of the damage done to *Akron*'s tail by a mooring accident. Notice the auxiliary steering station that could be used if the forward control car was out of action.

an upward draught of a great revolving air mass. Now the altimeter wobbled and the turbulent air shook the great airship before letting her drop back towards the water.

In the control car they ordered the engines to full speed. They were still falling, and the elevator man turned his wheel to maximum climb, and everyone prayed that the altimeter would stop. Barometric pressure meant nothing in such a swirling air mass. In the centre of a low-pressure region, the altimeter could have been 600 feet in error.

The altimeter showed 800 feet as the next shock came. Its vibration rang through the whole structure but it was no worse than many of the previous gusts. 'I was waiting for the shock of the stern hitting the water but it never came,' said the executive officer afterwards.

But it *had* come. With elevators set to climb, the airship's tail had swung low enough through the air to strike the wave tops.

Suddenly, with 300 feet on the altimeter, icy black waves came crashing through the windows of the control car. The lower part of the tail had been ripped off by the impact. As if to render the *coup de grâce*, a cross-wind rolled the airship enough for her belly to hit the water too. Hammered under the wind, the airship broke her back and the water

Far left: This dramatic photograph must be a reconstruction. That night the airship sank within minutes of hitting the water. Only 3 survivors were found. The forward section looks like the wreckage of the *Shenandoah* (shown on page 50).

Left: The control car of the *Akron* being lifted upside down from the sea by salvage teams.

61

roared into her.

There was virtually no life-saving gear aboard the *Akron*. In the Atlantic ocean that night even strong swimmers had little chance against the big waves and the cold that froze them to the bone. Of 76 men on *Akron*, only 3 were saved.

«ZR5.MACON» A survivor was the captain.

Just three mourning-filled weeks after *Akron* slid into the dark waters of the Atlantic, her sister ship *Macon* made her first flight. This airship was even more modern; none of her gas cells was made from gold-beater's skin – the delicate, animal intestine used for half of *Akron*'s cells and for those of most airships before her – instead a new gelatine-latex fabric was used. And *Macon* was faster, with marginally more useful lift.

The first sign of trouble for *Macon* came when she was one year old. Ordered to fly across the USA, the mountains of Arizona forced the airship up as high as 6,000 feet. Her 'pressure height' was less than 3,000 feet, so she lost a considerable amount of helium. To compensate, the airship dropped 9,000 lbs of ballast and then 7,000 lbs' weight of fuel. The airship remained too heavy but she would need all the rest of the fuel for the journey. Rather than resort to emergency measures, the helmsman brought the elevators to a climb position while the captain ordered the engines to cruising speed. This kept the slightly heavy airship at a constant altitude. Most of the text books categorised such flying as undesirable but the airship was flying through dangerous country, and by keeping his engine power the captain could follow the twists and turns of the canyons and of the heights that rose on either side of them.

Flying at such an up-angle creates stresses and strains on the framework but the new American airships were exceedingly tough and they could take it. But when, over Texas, the airship encountered the added torture of air turbulence, something had to give.

Most of the strain from flight at an up-angle centres upon the horizontal fins of the tailplane. At the place where the port-side fin was bolted to the airship, the ring buckled and two girders broke.

The design of the American rigids enabled all parts of the airship to be inspected during flight. The damage suffered over Texas was spotted immediately and the framework was reinforced. When the airship reached her destination, experts from the BuAer and Goodyear Zeppelin came to pronounce upon the breakage.

The verdict was that all four fins, and the ring to which they were attached, should be strengthened but that the work could be done piecemeal as operating schedules permitted. By February 1935 the work was almost complete. The top fin had been left to last, because that one alone would require the deflation of the two rearmost gas cells. That would be done in March.

On 12 February 1935, *Macon* was off the west coast of the USA where she had been on exercises with the Pacific Fleet. She was heading north along the coast of California towards her base at Sunny-

Commander Herbert V. Wiley, one of the only three survivors of the *Akron* disaster, was captain of the *Macon* when that crashed into the sea two years later.

Left: The *Macon* was one of the finest airships that ever flew. Inside her there was a hangar and aircraft came and went during the flight. Here *Macon* is seen over New York City.

vale near San Francisco. The sky darkened as the afternoon came, and by the time Point Sur was on the starboard bow, the mountains there were cloaked in fog. By now rain was drumming on the airship's cover and the wind was blustery and unpredictable, the way it is before a thunderstorm.

There was no other warning of the gust of wind that crippled her. It was a cross-wind, striking the airship with such force that the upper fin of the tail was knocked off, and took a part of the ring with it.

In the control car, the helmsman didn't know why the wheel suddenly went slack until he felt the airship sag by the tail. The ragged ends of metal had stabbed into the rearmost gas cells. They were leaking, and rain poured in through the flapping tears in the cover.

They reacted quickly in the control car – too quickly perhaps. No sooner had the telephones begun to report the damage, than hands reached for the ballast toggles. The captain this day was Wiley, executive officer of *Akron* that awful night only ten months previously, the only officer to escape from her alive.

They pulled the toggles and discharged 32,700 lbs of ballast and fuel. Whether by accident or design, they had exactly compensated for the lost lift from the deflated cells (between 30,000 and 40,000 lbs). Now the airship was in equilibrium, and with care might have been flown home. But *Macon* was tail-heavy and her engines were at cruising speed. Pointing skywards the airship climbed into the air and kept going. At 'pressure height', 2,800 feet, the automatic valves began discharging the helium, and continued to do so faster and faster all the way up to 4,850 feet.

Now there could be no chance of saving *Macon*. She was no longer a lighter-than-air machine; and it was surprising that her crew kept her in the sky a further twenty minutes.

Macon settled lightly into the water. The impact was gentle enough for men to dive from the airship into the water. Even the men in the control car were able to get out before the hull struck the ocean. Then, struggling to stay alive, *Macon* came nose first up out of the sea again, and stayed there tilted skywards. Sailors trapped inside the nose portion, knifed their way out through the cover. But such was the size of these monster airships that they were too high to dive into the water. While they waited for the leaking gas cells to settle the airship lower in the water, the gas caused the men to speak in very high voices (helium affects the vocal cords) so that the last men off the totally wrecked airship were laughing hysterically.

The water was not cold and there were ships nearby. The airship was plentifully equipped with life-saving gear. Of the 76 men on the last flight of *Macon*, only 2 were lost.

«HINDENBURG. LZ129»

Fire at Lakehurst. By 1936 the Zeppelin company had no rivals as designers, builders and operators of rigid airships. As well as her famous flights – round the world, to the Arctic, Middle East and eastern Europe – the *Graf Zeppelin* airship had established a regular passenger service between Germany and South America. As 1936 ended, *Graf Zeppelin* had flown a grand total of 1 million kilometres, 16,000 flying hours in 578 successful flights.

But *Graf Zeppelin* had been made to fit the small hangar at Friedrichshafen; she was not suited to the rigours and distances of the North Atlantic, although she had braved them a few times.

Hindenburg was designed and built for the route to New York. The enormous size of the new German airship was partly due to the expectation that

The airships carried mail and the *Hindenburg* had a post office working during its flights. This is a typical rubber stamp used on such mail.

the USA would share its helium monopoly. (This non-inflammable gas was less efficient in lift.) The *Hindenburg* was not only the biggest airship known until then, she was the biggest flying machine the world has known, before or since: a giant Boeing 707 airliner could have been hidden under *Hindenburg*'s tailplane.

The hope that the US government would permit the export of helium was in vain. The *Hindenburg* was inflated with hydrogen and yet the expectation of helium had provided the airship with a fatal legacy. The use of some hydrogen in *Hindenburg* was in any case a part of the original design. The hydrogen cells were to be positioned inside the helium bags, to provide cheaper gas that could be valved off without wasting expensive helium. It was this idea that resulted in automatic valves, and the manually operated ones, positioned right in the centre of the hull. Access to them was by a walkway that went all the way through the exact centre of the airship. The gas from the valves went up through long 'chimneys' to the top of the envelope.

During 1936 *Hindenburg* made ten scheduled flights to New York (Lakehurst) and seven to Rio. During the lay-off period of the winter of 1936–7, the added lift provided by the hydrogen made it possible to add nine more cabins to the passenger space. When the airship left her new base at Frankfurt on 3 May 1937, on her way to Lakehurst, this was the first of eighteen flights scheduled for this route in a year that would include the coronation of George VI and the Paris Exposition. There was no other passenger service across the Atlantic by air except the airship flights that had, for seven years, linked Germany with Brazil, and now the new service to the USA. And the Zeppelin company could still boast that not one farepaying passenger had ever been killed or injured in one of their airships.

Hindenburg left Rhein-Main airport at 8 p.m. car-

Left: *Hindenburg* flies over the Zeppelin Field at the end of the Nazi Party Congress in Nuremberg, 1936.

Right: The fire that began near the tail raced through the ventilation shafts

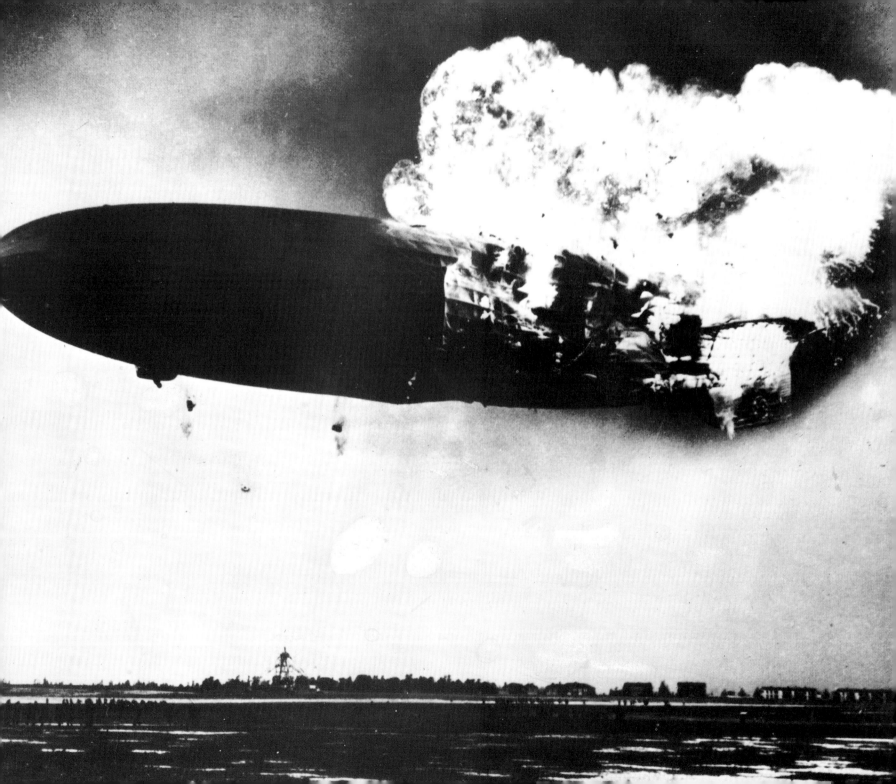

rying 36 passengers. As well as the three captains normally carried for the three-watch system, two other experienced captains were also aboard. The normal crew, of about 40, was brought up to 61 by the inclusion of many trainees who were being prepared for a sister airship, at that time being built (LZ130 – *Graf Zeppelin II*).

Hindenburg passed over Cologne, where mail was dropped, and then went over the Netherlands to the North Sea, heading westwards through the Pas de Calais, without sighting the French or English coast due to poor visibility. The airship used the shortest route, via Newfoundland, and flew low so that the passengers would see the giant icebergs. The airship was not subjected to any turbulence during the journey, but stiff headwinds of up to 50 m.p.h. forced the captain to radio that he would be delayed; instead of 6 a.m. on 6 May he would land at 6 p.m. The *Hindenburg* arrived over the airship base at Lakehurst about 4 p.m. At about that time, a cold front accompanied by thunderstorms was approaching, so the airship cruised a few miles to the south to avoid the brunt of the bad weather. Because of this, *Hindenburg* did not come in to land until 7 p.m., thirteen hours later than scheduled.

The mooring party, of over 200 men, watched the airship pass over at about 600 feet so that the men on the airship could see the surface conditions. She circled and then came in for the landing, dropping ballast and valving hydrogen to adjust the trim. Headed into wind, the airship sank to 200 feet and then reversed the engines to check the forward speed. It was 7.21 p.m. as the manila landing ropes were thrown from the airship to the rain-shiny ground. The rain was very light by now and the last rays of the sun were diffused by thin clouds.

Passengers were crowded at the windows, especially those on the starboard side, from which they might be able to see friends and relatives waiting for them. Passenger baggage had been brought out of the cabins and left in the passageways ready to be off-loaded.

The mooring party, virtually all experienced men, took the manila lines and connected them to ground lines. Then the steel mooring cable began to come from the airship's nose.

In the control car some men had noticed a tail-heaviness that had persisted for over half-an-hour. Now they all felt a shudder run through the airship's frame. The captain looked at the instruments – there was no sign of trouble and the gas cells were all at normal pressure.

However, crew in the tail saw fire. The axial walkway went exactly through the middle of the airship. At a place near the tail (where gas cell number 4 met gas cell number 5) there was both a ventilation shaft upwards, and a ladder down to the keel. It was here that one of the crew heard 'a muffled detonation and saw from the starboard side, down inside the gas cell, a bright reflection through and inside the cell.'

The ventilation shaft, and the valves that vented into them, had originally been a part of the design for a hydrogen plus helium combination airship. Now the fire roared up the shaft, igniting any last traces of gas that remained from the landing manoeuvres, and a flicker of it was seen by the crowd watching the landing.

The flames appeared just forward of the upper fin. As the gas was burned away, the tail – already slightly heavy – dropped. Every natural instinct for an airship-man was to discharge ballast and bring the airship up again. With an amazing speed and clarity of thought, they did not do this. They stood by their controls as the tail section, a blazing torch by this time, crashed to the ground. This decision enabled some of those aboard to scramble out

Right: At this moment someone in the control cabin must have decided to let the flaming tail sink to the ground. This saved many lives.

before the flames got to them.

Tail on the ground, *Hindenburg* bent in the middle as the nose tilted steeply upwards. The axial walkway now became a chimney, and out of the tip of the airship's nose there poured a long jet of flame. Then the whole front section collapsed back to earth, crushing the two-level passenger and crew accommodation under a tangle of flaming wreckage.

Men and women escaped, even from this inferno. One elderly lady walked out by the normal exit as though nothing had happened and was unscratched. A 14-year-old cabin boy jumped to the ground into flames and smoke. He was almost unconscious from the fumes when a water-ballast bag collapsed over his head. He got out. One passenger hacked his way through a jungle of hot metal, using his bare hands. Another emerged safely, only to have another passenger land upon him and cripple him. One man, at an open window with every chance to jump to safety, went back into the flames to his wife – both died.

The flames continued for over three hours, due to the tons of diesel fuel that were aboard at the time of the crash. Amazingly, 62 of the 97 people on board survived the disaster.

Of all airship crashes *Hindenburg*'s remains the most mysterious and the most contentious. Many theorists were attracted to the idea of sabotage. An incendiary device could have been positioned at the place the fire started. There was an access ladder there (from the keel) as well as a ventilation shaft to fan the flames.

The most attractive aspect of the sabotage theory is the timing. Had the airship arrived on time at 6 o'clock in the morning a bomb timed for after 7 p.m. would not have caused the horrifying casualties. In the absence of any real evidence to support the theory, some have been tempted to provide the

villain instead. Max Pruss, captain at the time of the crash, eventually came to suspect a certain passenger. Others have chosen members of the crew. But not only did the American investigators fail to find any evidence of sabotage, the Gestapo investigation was equally negative. Unconvinced by this, some of the sabotage theorists have made the whole thing into a Nazi plot.

Many explanations fit the circumstances without recourse to the sensational solutions. The presence of free hydrogen deep inside the ship can be attributed to various causes; the valves that were placed along the axial walkway (one expert suggested that the valve at cell 4 might have stuck open). The very slow approach-speed of the airship, after valving gas, might well have left some gas residue in the shafts. The tail heaviness, noticed by the elevator man, might have been the result of a gas leak, and that had been in evidence for half-an-hour, enough time for a great deal of gas to collect in the tail.

The only other necessary ingredient is the spark. Both American and German investigators agreed that some form of static discharge was the source of the fire. One expert on electrostatics and atmospheric electricity said that the manila ropes dropped to the ground would have been enough

to make the airship discharge electricity, and continue to so do for some minutes.

One witness has been found (by Dr Robinson, the noted airship historian) who testifies to seeing the dim blue light of St Elmo's fire on the top of the airship before the flames appeared.

Dr Eckener, perhaps the greatest airship expert, believed that the *Hindenburg*'s last turn had overstressed the hull, and that this snapped a bracing wire. This steel wire would have cut the gas cells like a razor. Eckener's theory was supported by the very sharp turn the airship had made, when reacting to a wind change, and the tension gauges salvaged from the wreckage. These showed that the 'bicycle spoke' wires bracing the rings had been at very high tension.

In June 1974 I spoke about the *Hindenburg* disaster with Captain Hans von Schiller who, at the time of the disaster, was the captain of the *Graf Zeppelin* airship, flying back from South America. Reluctant to commit himself to any theory, von Schiller made the following comments. His vast experience of airships, and his keen mind, provide what I believe to be the most probable explanation of the crash.

No one can say. Pruss and Lehmann were the finest of airship commanders, men of vast experience. But maybe, I say maybe, when they were landing, a tail wind blew back along the ventilation system. There were always a few leaks of hydrogen. Air blowing from behind would prevent it escaping. Now, when an airship lands it reverses its engines, just as a ship does. And, like a ship, it vibrates. Now I'm not saying this happened, I am saying maybe. But if the Zeppelin vibrates so much, it could break a wire. These bracing wires are thick, and when they snap, heat is generated at the break. Now if the hot end of the wire recoiled into the build-up of leaking gas, this could have caused the fire.

Dr Hugo Eckener had captained the *Hindenburg* on its early trans-Atlantic flights.

Far Left: A walkway went right through the middle of the *Hindenburg*. Flame raced through this passage and burst through the nose.

Left: The burnt-out remains of the *Hindenburg*.

«GRAF ZEPPELIN. LZ130»

The last Zeppelin. When Ernst Lehmann, by now Flight Director of the Zeppelin company, staggered away from the burning *Hindenburg* severely burned, he said, 'I don't understand it, I don't understand it.' He was echoing the thoughts of the whole world. Just when the airship seemed to have established herself as a safe, reliable, commercially viable way to travel – and the only way to cross the Atlantic by air – the disaster at Lakehurst came.

Appalled by the well-documented horror, many Americans felt guilty about the export ban on helium. Now there were high expectations of changes in the law, to permit Germany to use helium in *Hindenburg*'s sister ship, due to be finished building in 1938.

At the time of *Hindenburg*'s fiery end, *Graf Zeppelin* was in the air, returning from her scheduled service between Germany and Brazil. Her captain, Hans von Schiller, received the terrible news through the airship's radio officer but decided not to tell his passengers. When the *Graf Zeppelin* landed at Friedrichshafen her passengers were not only the last fare-payers to travel on a rigid airship, they were just about the last people in the civilised world to hear about the *Hindenburg*'s end.

Graf Zeppelin made only one more flight. On 18 June 1937 she lifted off from her home at Friedrichshafen and circled the airfield twice before going to Frankfurt to be deflated and used solely as an exhibit. It had long been decided that the airship would be de-commissioned by 1939, and she had already flown an unprecedentedly long time. And the gas capacity of *Graf Zeppelin* was such that the poorer performance of helium as a lifting gas would have made it an unsuitable fuel for her transatlantic service to Brazil.

By the summer of 1938, *Hindenburg*'s sister ship was almost complete and already modified for operation on hydrogen. Some believed that US government permission for the export of helium to Germany might coincide with the centennial of the Count's birth on 8 July 1938. But, in spite of the approval of President Roosevelt and the military, the export of helium was deliberately blocked by the Secretary of the Interior. The negligible military worth of helium suggests that this was simply a political gesture designed to look like a blow against fascism. (In fact, each ocean crossing used up over 5 per cent of the helium gas. The LZ130's flying programme would have ended as soon as the USA ceased supplying the helium.)

The LZ130, now named *Graf Zeppelin*, flew only about thirty times, and never carried fare-paying passengers. Used as a flying electronics laboratory she was sent to the English coast to check radar wave-lengths but failed to do so. The conspicuous airship had no real military value, and as soon as war began she was deflated. In May 1940, as the German armoured divisions invaded France and the Low Countries, Hermann Göring ordered a Luftwaffe construction battalion to dynamite the sheds at Frankfurt, and demolish both *Graf Zeppelin* airships. The era of the rigid airship had ended.

Right: Alfred Eisenstaedt was allowed only a few minutes in which to get no more than three pictures of repairs being made to the fabric of the hydrogen-filled hull of the *Graf Zeppelin*. This remarkable photograph was taken over the South Atlantic during a scheduled passenger flight.

ACKNOWLEDGMENTS

Hans von Schiller

As this book was completed I was grieved to hear of the death of Kapitän Hans von Schiller who had helped me considerably with the preparation of the text. After flying in 14 different airships von Schiller (above) ended his career as captain of the *Graf Zeppelin*. His death marks the end of an era, and I hope this book might be a token thanks for his great help and many kindnesses.

I must also thank Douglas Robinson, that doyen of airship historians, who generously provided me with advice and photographs. So did Kurt Puzicha of the Marine Luftschiffer Kameradschaft (Naval Airship Old Comrades Association) who opened that archive to me. In London Cyril Sharpe gave me free access to his particularly fine collection of photographs, while John McK. Tucker tracked down some little-known pictures in the USA. At her office in Old Brewer's Yard, London, Annie Horton, a picture researcher with considerable knowledge of airships, assembled hundreds of pictures – some of them very rare – from which Arnold Schwartzman, the designer of the book, Tony Colwell of Cape, and I, after much deliberation, chose those that are reproduced here. For permission to print them I also thank Associated Press; the Robert Hunt Library; Illustrated London News; the Imperial War Museum, London; Popperfoto; the Press Association; the Radio Times Hulton Picture Library; the Royal Aeronautical Society; Syndication International; Time-Life Inc; United Press International; the US National Archives; as well as the Bildarchiv Preussischer Kulturbesitz in Berlin; Süddeutscher Verlag, Munich; and Ullstein Bilderdienst, Berlin. The John Frost Newspaper Library came up with the cuttings which have been reproduced in the book with the permission of the proprietors of the *Daily Mirror*, the *Philadelphia Inquirer* and the *Columbus Evening Dispatch*.

For reading the text and offering helpful additions, I am grateful to Hans Schlotter of Bad Oeyhausen, Geschäftsführer of ArGe Zeppelinpost, of which I am a member. I should also like to thank my fellow members of the Lighter Than Air Society of Akron, Ohio, and the Zeppelin Collectors' Club. Thanks also to Donald S. Lopez of the Smithsonian, Washington.

For further reading I strongly recommend *Giants in the Sky* (Foulis, London, 1973) and *Zeppelin in Combat* (Foulis, London, 1971) both by Douglas Robinson.

Other books that I have found useful include *The British Rigid Airship 1908–1931* by Robin Higham (Foulis, London, 1962); *Ships in the Sky* by John Toland (Muller, London, 1957); *Historic Airships* by Peter W. Brooks (Evelyn, London, 1973); *The Achievement of the Airship* by G. Hartcup (David & Charles, Newton Abbot, 1961); *Zeppelin, Wegbereiter des Weltluftverkehrs* by Kapitän Hans von Schiller (Kirschbaumverlag, Bad Godesberg, 1966); *Zeppelins Over England* by K. Poolman (Evans Bros, London, 1960); *Zeppelins Over England* by Baron von Buttlar Brandenfels (Harrap, London, 1931) from which I quote on p. 27; *The Zeppelin Fighters* by A. Whitehouse (Robert Hale, London, 1968); *Zeppelin Adventures* by Rolf Marben (John Hamilton, London, 1931); *The Life of Barnes Wallis* by J. E. Morpurgo (Longmans, London, 1972); *The Airships 'Akron' & 'Macon'* by Richard K. Smith (Naval Institute Press, Maryland, USA, 1965); *Les Ballons* by Charles Dollfus (Robert Delpire, Paris, 1960).

I have also used material from a speech given by Mr Smith at the Smithsonian in Washington, D.C., in 1968.

A VISUAL GLOSSARY OF TECHNICAL TERMS

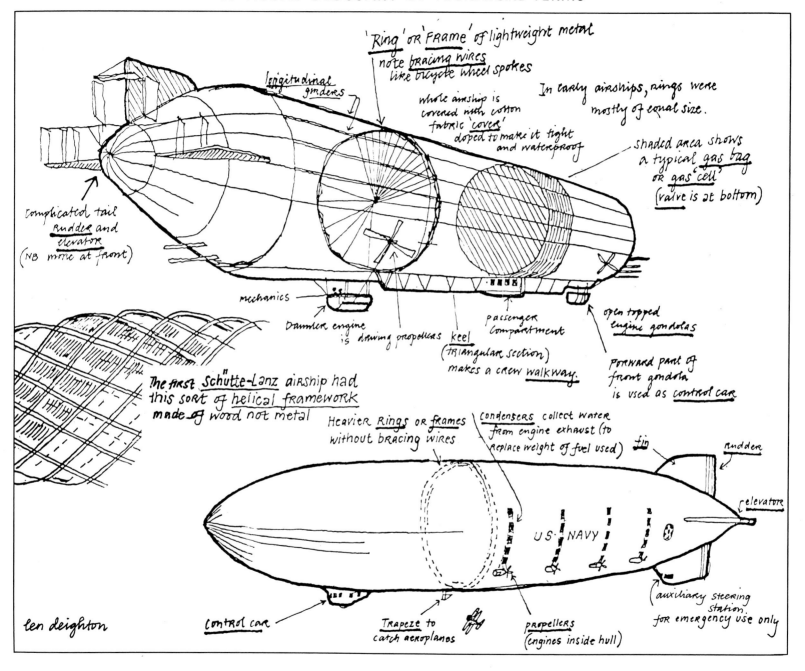

'Ring' or 'Frame' of lightweight metal
note bracing wires
like bicycle wheel spokes

In early airships, rings were mostly of equal size.

longitudinal girders

whole airship is covered with cotton fabric 'cover' doped to make it tight and waterproof

shaded area shows a typical gas bag or gas 'cell' (valve is at bottom)

complicated tail Rudder and elevator (NB more at front)

mechanics

Daimler engine is driving propellers

keel (triangular section) makes a crew walkway.

passenger compartment

open topped engine gondolas

forward part of front gondola is used as control car

The first Schütte-Lanz airship had this sort of helical framework made of wood not metal

Heavier Rings or frames without bracing wires

condensers collect water from engine exhaust (to replace weight of fuel used)

rudder

elevator

U.S. NAVY

auxiliary steering station for emergency use only

len deighton

control car

Trapeze to catch aeroplanes

propellers (engines inside hull)

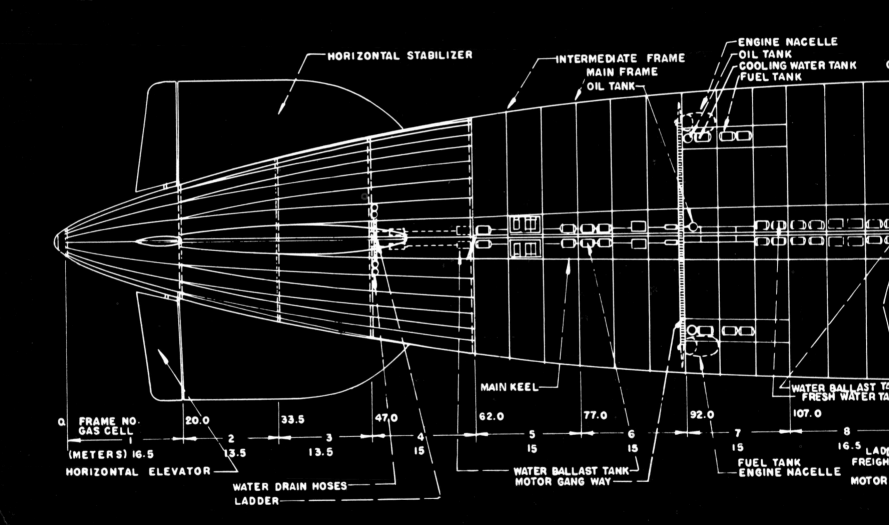

HORIZONTAL STABILIZER

INTERMEDIATE FRAME
MAIN FRAME
OIL TANK

ENGINE NACELLE
OIL TANK
COOLING WATER TANK
FUEL TANK

MAIN KEEL

WATER BALLAST TA
FRESH WATER TA

Q	FRAME NO.	20.0	33.5	47.0	62.0	77.0	92.0	107.0	
	GAS CELL								
	1	2	3	4	5	6	7	8	
(METERS)	16.5	13.5	13.5	15	15	15	15	16.5	

LADDER
FREIGH

HORIZONTAL ELEVATOR

WATER DRAIN HOSES
LADDER

WATER BALLAST TANK
MOTOR GANG WAY

FUEL TANK
ENGINE NACELLE

MOTOR